E. WARREN CLARK'S 1878
LIFE AND ADVENTURE
IN JAPAN

LIFE AND ADVENTURE IN JAPAN

E. WARREN CLARK'S 1878 LIFE AND ADVENTURE IN JAPAN

edited By Daniel A. Metraux and Jessica Puglisi

Writers Club Press

San Jose   New York   Lincoln   Shanghai

E. WARREN CLARK'S 1878
LIFE AND ADVENTURE IN JAPAN

Writers Club Press
an imprint of iUniverse, Inc.

For information address:
iUniverse, Inc.
5220 S. 16th St., Suite 200
Lincoln, NE 68512
www.iuniverse.com

"See early Japan from the inside!"

ISBN: 0-595-21587-4

Printed in the United States of America

Dedication

This book is dedicated to:

For Daniel Metraux: Dr. John Shayne and the Nursing Staff at Augusta Medical Center who saved my life; my loving and wonderful wife Judy who nursed me back to health; our beautiful adult children Katie and David; Susilee Reynolds Scherer (1948-2001); marvelous student teaching assistants Lin Lin Aung, Cara Costigan, Jessica Puglisi, Jaime Curley; former students really "making it" in the world—Veronica Vicente, Margaret Richardson, Tarah Blazek, and Anne-Louise Lasley and her baby; my second "father" and mentor, Wilton S. Dillon; my god-mother and teacher, Margaret Mead; our parents, Rhoda and Alfred Metraux and Lillian and Russell Menelly; Jeffrey Buller and Cynthia Tyson for their constant support.; and to Prof. Ben Dorman with the hope that our book together will be a shining success.

For Jessica D. Puglisi: To my family with thanks for all their love and support.

Contents

Dedication v
Preface ix
Chronology xi
FIRST INTRODUCTION 3
SECOND INTRODUCTION 23
Chapter 1
    First Sight of Japan 27
Chapter 2
    A Journey on the "Tokaido" 34
Chapter 3
    Life In A Buddhist Temple 45
Chapter 4
    Life in a Feudal Castle 57
Chapter Five
    Excursions and Comical Experiences 71
Chapter 6
    The Ascent Of Fuji-Yama. 85
Chapter 7
    Removal to Tokyo 104
Chapter 8
    Rambles About the Capital 116
Chapter 9
    A Peep into the Mikado's Palace 130
Chapter 10
    A Trip to Kyoto 140
Chapter 11
    The Missionary Outlook 157
Chapter 12
    Farewell to Japan 167

AFTERWORD 178
About the Author 187
Bibliography 189

Preface

E. Warren Clark's 1878 book, *Life and Adventure in Japan*, is an exquisite portrait of Japan in the early 1870s. Japan at that time had just opened itself to the West for the first time and had only recently commenced a vigorous process of modernization that would soon transform a quaint isolated kingdom into a modern superpower. Clark's work presents the reader with one of the best opportunities available to gain a fascinating in-person view of Japan during this critical age.

E. Warren Clark (1849-1907) was one of many American and European teachers and expert technicians hired by the Japanese to help them become a modern industrial and military power. The Japanese hoped to become strong enough to protect their independence against what they perceived as the menacing imperial power of the West in the late 1800s. Clark was one of many teachers who taught hundreds of young Japanese the rudiments of modern science. It is ironic that today the Japanese government's well-funded JET (Japan Exchange and Teaching) Program continues this process by hiring several thousand young Americans, Europeans and other English-speaking foreigners every year to teach in Japanese schools.

After his return from Japan Clark wrote three books and many articles about his Japan experience, but it is his *Life and Adventure in Japan* that gives his freshest and most comprehensive view. Unfortunately, Clark has been largely forgotten by modern scholars and his book has been out of print for over a century. It is hoped that the republication of this work will reintroduce Clark and his view of Japan to new generations of scholars.

This writer discovered Clark's book in an old barn in Barton, Vermont in 1975 and bought it for a mere 35 cents. This find led to a research trip to Japan in the summer of 1985 and a presentation at an international conference, The *Yatoi—A Comprehensive Study of Hired Foreigners,* held in Fukui city, Japan in October 1985. This writer's paper, "The Role of the *Oyatoi Gaikokujin* in the development of Mutual Images Between Alien Cultures: The Work of Edward Warren Clark," was later published in a Japanese book that served as the proceedings of the conference.

This writer wishes to thank his brilliant student and teaching assistant, Jessica Puglisi, for all her typing and other work that has hopefully rescued Clark from oblivion. Thanks also to another TA, Lin Lin Aung, a truly brilliant Burmese student who has done so much to help my work as well as that of my wife Judy.

The Year 2001 was a dark year not only for our nation, but also for my family. My mother, Rhoda Metraux, my father-in-law, Russell Menelly, and I suffered near fatal illnesses while our closest friend, Susilee Reynolds Scherer (1948-2001) died after a long fight with cancer. Judy and her mother, Lillian Menelly, literally nursed us back to health. I want to dedicate this work to Jessica, Lin Lin, Lillian and, most especially, Judy without whose loving care life would have little meaning and joy. Special thanks also to Dr. John Shayne, the kind, gentle and very skilled surgeon who literally saved my life, and to the many wonderful patient nurses at Augusta Medical Center (near Staunton VA) who cared for me after two critical operations.

Co-editor Jessica D. Puglisi wishes to dedicate this book "To my family, with thanks for all their loving support."

And finally thanks to our new Dean, Dr. Jeffrey Buller, for the encourage-ment he has given the faculty towards the advancement of their research.

Daniel A. Metraux
Mary Baldwin College
Staunton, VA
Winter 2002

Chronology

Japan's Meiji Period: 1868-1912
E. Warren Clark: Born in Portsmouth, NH in 1849: Died in 1907
Clark's Visits to Japan: 1871-75; 1895; and 1904
First Publication of Clark's *Life and Adventure in Japan*: 1878
Publication of Clark's *Katz Awa: "The Bismarck of Japan"*: 1904
Russo-Japanese War: 1904-05

E. WARREN CLARK'S 1878 LIFE AND ADVENTURE IN JAPAN

FIRST INTRODUCTION

JAPANESE-AMERICAN RELATIONS IN THE MEIJI ERA: CONFLICTING MISCONCEIVED IMAGES

By Daniel A. Metraux
Mary Baldwin College

Japan during the period between 1868 to 1945 was very fearful of being overwhelmed by the might of the West. The Japanese, attempting to become as powerful as or even stronger than most Western powers, transformed itself from a small weak feudal state into an industrialized nation by learning and adopting from the West whatever was necessary to build a Rich Nation and a Strong Army (*fukoku kyoohei*) and to Civilize and Enlighten (*bummei kaika*). To facilitate this process the Japanese government hired several thousand foreign teachers, technologists, and advisors (*oyatoi gaikokujin;* literally, "hired foreigners") during the Meiji Period (1868-1912) to provide wide expertise in fields in which it was felt that the West excelled. The subject of this introduction, E. Warren Clark (1849-1907), was hired because of his experience in natural sciences, especially chemistry. The Japanese drive to modernize set the context of its relationships with the United States and other Western powers.

The United States has enjoyed a close but often stormy relationship with Japan since the arrival of Commodore Perry's "Black Ships" in 1853. The two nations have shared a mutual fascination and respect for each other, but misconceptions about the other's identity, power and intentions have often nurtured intense levels of mistrust and conflict. The irony is that despite nearly 150 years of close contact, both nations persist in talking at rather than with each other and advance national interest over shared responsibility.

Many educated "Gilded Age" Americans believed that civilization and progress were inseparable from Anglo-Saxon heritage and Christianity. Early American visitors to Japan, many of them missionaries and teachers, arrived with the preconceived notion that the United States represented the pinnacle of "civilization" because of its cultivation of "a democratic society of Christian principles, commercial wealth and technological innovation....Missionaries, scholars, and artists [who] made Japan a perennial and popular topic in Gilded-Age media...arrived in Japan[1] convinced of white, Christian superiority." [2]

---

[1] After returning from his successful venture to open Japan in 1854 , Commodore Matthew Perry wrote:

> Viewed in any of its aspects, the Empire of Japan has long presented to the thoughtful mind an object of uncommon interest.....The man of commerce asks to be told of its products,...the commodities it needs, and the returns it can supply...The ethnologist is curious to pry into the physical appearance of its inhabitants; to dig, if possible, from its fossil remains of long buried history; and in the affiliation of its people to supply, perchance, a gap in the story of man's early wanderings over the globe. ...The Christian desires to know the varied of their superstition and idolatry; and longs for the dawn of that day when a purer faith and more enlightened worship shall bring them within the circle of Christendom.

> Quoted in Thom Burns, "America's 'Japan': 1853-1952" in *Kyoto Journal (40) 1999*, p. 26.

[2] Joseph M Henning, *Outposts of Civilization: Race, Religion, and the Formative Years of American-Japanese Relations* (New York and London: New York University Press, 2000), pp. 2-4.

Joseph M. Henning, author of one of the best studies of Japanese-American relations in the Meiji Era (1868-1912), *Outposts of Civilization: Race, Religion, and the Formative Years of American-Japanese Relations,* introduces us to two young graduates of Rutgers University, E. Warren Clark and William E. Griffis (1843-1928).[3] These young men journeyed to Japan as teachers and lay missionaries in the early 1870s and later wrote books and articles and gave public lectures on Japan that helped to shape American opinions and images of the country in the late 19th and early 20th centuries. They came as young idealists imbued with the optimism and certainty of progress and as self-appointed teachers from what they regarded as a superior culture. The intellectual trend of their day had given up the preoccupation of a golden age in the past. Instead, the young Victorian thinkers looked to a future that promised progress toward a better world.

Indeed, at the time that Clark and Griffis went to Japan, this idea of progress had become a firmly held conviction in the United States and northern Europe. Western thinkers and practitioners relied on science, new technology and modern machinery that vastly expanded work capacity and promised an improved well-being for many. Such material benefits were also expected to enhance moral progress as well. Living under better conditions, it was assumed that human beings would better themselves. Such thoughts were closely entwined with the religious convictions of many educated people of the age who, like Clark and Griffis, were convinced that Christianity held the key to human progress and must serve as the foundation of the spread of the progressive Westernization of the non-Western world.

Like many other missionaries and educators in Japan at the time, Clark believed that education and Christianization were intertwined and that

---

[3] William Griffis, a classmate of Clark at Rutgers, spent several years in Japan as a teacher in Echizen (Fukui) and Tokyo. His famous and very lengthy book, *The Mikado's Empire,* went through many editions from the 1870s to the early 1900s. His book was considered the definitive word on Japanese history and culture for several decades.

one had to accompany the other. Clark and Griffis were among those who promoted the idea that Christianity was the main reason for the material success of the West and that backward Japanese attitudes toward life had to be replaced by a new outlook, compatible with the assumptions of Western science and based on the civilizing aspects of Christianity. They both had a profound sense of participating in a great Christian adventure – the evangelization of Japan.[4] Clark, like Griffis, felt that Japanese modernization was to be accomplished "ultimately through the acceptance of Christianity on the part of the Japanese people."[5] The key to liberation,

---

[4] It is interesting to note that several contemporary Japanese scholars also shared the utilitarian view that their country could only Westernize and Modernize if it simultaneously adopted Christianity.

See A. Hamish Ion, "Edward Warren Clark and Early Major Japan: Case Study of Cultural Contact" in *Modern Asian Studies,* II, 4 (1977), pp. 557-72. See esp. pp. 564-65 and 571.

Ion writes that Clark had had a profound effect on one young Japanese scholar, Nakamura Masano. Nakamura had first become acquainted with Christianity in England, where he had lived between 1866-68 as one of the supervisors to a group of 12 students sent there to study by the Tokugawa government. Nakamura felt that the appeal of Christianity was not spiritual, but principally due to its moral code. Ion notes:

> Shortly after meeting Clark, Nakamura wrote a memorial addressed to the Emperor urging toleration of Christianity. In it he stated that "the industry, patience and perseverance in their arts, inventions and machinery, all have their origin in the faith, hope and charity of their religion, and religion is the root and foundation on which their prosperity depends." Christianity, according to Nakamura, was the essence of Western civilization. In the memorial Nakamura even suggested that the Emperor should become Christian, for this act would improve Japan's relations with the West. The acceptance…was seen as a patriotic gesture which would materially benefit the country. The Western religion was seen as being utilitarian and practical in nature because it was the ultimate basis of Western strength.

[5] Watanabe Masao, "E. W. Kuraku: Beokokujin Kagaku Kyoshi" (E.W. Clark: American Science Teacher in Japan) in *Kagaku Kenkyu,* II.14 (116), 1975, p. 178.

notes Clark, was the wholesale importation of Western civilization along with its Christian foundation.

Clark and Griffis' faith, which was strongly influenced by the revivalist religious spirit of mid-nineteenth century New England, was rooted in the belief that God's work here on earth must be carried out by individuals acting in accordance with a high moral code and the dictates of their Christian consciences[6]. In much of his writing, Clark speaks of the need to impress the Japanese with his own high moral standards (including the refusal of the offer of a Japanese "wife.").

Henning notes that there had been a heated debate between the early 1870s and late 1890s between two camps of American writers over what is needed for a society to become civilized: "those [writers] who advocated secular and scientific progress and those who championed Christianity as the indispensable prerequisite for progress."[7] Missionaries and lay missionary teachers like Clark had preached that no country could be considered civilized without Christianity and that only the gospel provided the power to lift people out of the degradation. But as Japan made notable advances in technology and industrialization some secular visitors began to argue that Japan, now revived and open to the world, was aspiring and already advancing toward the higher level of civilization without Christianity.... In the early Meiji period, several American analysts noted that Japan had an ancient, refined, and dynamic civilization quite distinct from and in some respects superior to Western civilization: they found the Japanese an industrious, quick-witted and noble people. Even though Japan was assimilating Western ideas, many Americans acknowledged that it had a civilization of his own from which the West might learn. In this view, because Japan was already civilized, its assimilation of Western ideas was not necessarily an unadulterated improvement.[8]

---

[6] H. Paul Varley, *Japanese Culture* (New York: 1977), p. 176.

[7] Henning, p. 66.

[8] Ibid., pp. 64-65.

American missionaries were concerned in 1879 when British writer Edwin Arnold published his seminal work, *The Light of Asia*. Arnold's warm introduction to Buddhism sold a half million copies and created a very favorable image of the religion. American journalist Edward House, writing in the 1870s and 1880s, painted missionaries as being "curiously unintelligent and illiterate professors of a narrow and microscopic Christianity." (p. 76) Arnold and House approached the question of civilization and progress from the perspective of morality. The West, they claimed, had little if anything to teach the East about ethical behavior. Such claims brought strong denunciations in the missionary press in Japan and the United States.

Japan's rapid and successful transition into a major world power, however, forced even American missionaries and their supporters to come to grips with the Japanese phenomenon: a successful embrace by a non-Western people of modern civilization. Religious American writers like Clark and Griffis soon developed a hearty respect for the politeness, cleanliness, intelligence, devotion to work, and high ethical standards of the Japanese. They reconciled the seeming contradiction between Japan's obvious achievements and its high degree of civilization and the fact that by the Russo-Japanese War (1904-05), Japan had not transformed itself into a Christian country by saying that Japan had all of the *latent tendencies* of an Anglo-Saxon Christian country.

The War represents the highpoint of favorable American attitudes towards Japan before Pearl Harbor. American missionary writers portrayed Japan as a most progressive and modern nation, which alone amongst the nations of Asia had the potential of adopting the Anglo-Saxon traditions of the West. The fact that Christianity had found few converts was not terribly disturbing in itself because Japanese had been found to possess such latent tendencies such as honesty, self-sacrifice, patience, hard work and grace. Having these qualities together with the science and technology of the West made the eventual conversion to Christianity a virtual certainty.

This enthusiastic image of Japan is best portrayed in the writing of Sidney Gulick, a Japan-based missionary, teacher and historian during the latter years of the Meiji period. Gulick's book, *The White Peril in the Far East*,[9] which was written at the height of the Russo-Japanese War, is a blanket indictment of the Russians as an enemy of progressive Western civilization. Gulick's ideas were strongly echoed in the writings and sentiments of other writers like Clark and Griffis and in the thinking and policies of many politicians like President Theodore Roosevelt.

Gulick urged Americans to support the "progressive" Japanese as they fought for their survival against the "regressive" Russian empire. Gulick comments that although few Japanese had converted to Christianity while most Russians were at least nominally Christian, the Japanese boasted such modern and Christian values as honesty, progressivism, democracy, education, and openness towards the Western church. Gulick stressed that one must regard Japan as a most "virtuous country" because of its highly enthusiastic reception of and adaptation to Western and "Anglo-Saxon" values. The Russians, on the other hand, are regarded as a genuine menace to world peace. They are aggressive, uneducated, dishonest, and reactionary. A Russian victory over Japan would thus be a major defeat for those progressive forces in the West who sought a new world order based on reason and science.

Gulick literally saw the Russo-Japanese war as a conflict between the forces of good and evil, progress and reaction. Nominally Christian Russia represented very "unchristian" tendencies while Japan, though not in any technical sense a Christian country, possessed all of the "virtues" of Christianity. Gulick warned that Japan was the West's one hope for the successful implantation of Western Christian civilization in Asia and that American support for Japan was critical for the success of this endeavor.

---

[9] Sidney L. Gulick, *The White Peril in the Far East* (New York, 1905).

These incredibly pro-Japanese feelings for Japan, however, dissipated soon after the War. Japan's victory over Russia made it a world power and a presumed threat to other imperialist powers in Asia. American leaders began to ponder the weakness of their position in the Philippines and Hawaii and the hostility of white Californians to growing Japanese immigration to the West Coast. The favorable image of Japan spawned by American writers like Gulick, Griffis and Clark swiftly vanished in the mist of the growing antagonism and mistrust that eventually led to Pearl Harbor and the Pacific War of 1941-45.

THE JAPAN AMERICA INVENTED

It is time that a writer treated Japan as something else than an Oriental puzzle, a nation of recluses, a land of fabulous wealth, of universal licentiousness or of Edenic purity, the fastness of a treacherous and fickle crew, a Paradise of guileless children, a Utopia of artists and poets. It is time to drop the license of exaggeration, and, with the light of common day, yet with sympathy and without prejudice, seek to know what Dai Nippon is and has been.

William Griffis, 1876[10]

Oscar Wilde noted sarcastically in 1889 that "…Japan is a pure invention. There is no such country, there are no such people."[11] Wilde was responding to the Western infatuation with Japan at the time. The West had developed such an extreme enthusiasm for traditional Japanese arts and imagery known as *japonisme* that various American writers concluded that Japan was rapidly becoming the veritable "Anglo-Saxon" and "latently

---

[10] Quoted in Burns, p. 24
[11] Quoted in Burns, p. 25.

Christian" nation through its rapid adoption of Western technology and institutions.

American writers of the nineteenth century presented a complex and on occasion contradictory portrait of Japan that "divulges more about the values, mores and norms of their own society than about the distant land they glossed over."[12] The "quaintness" of Japanese culture contrasted greatly with its explosive modernization. While other Asian nations such as China appeared lost in a quagmire of tradition, Japan had begun "…erecting factories, …conscripting an army, …preparing a parliament. There were universities, offices, department stores, (and) banks."[13] Japan's sudden emergence as a modern power drew accolades from all quarters and encouraged writers to mold Japan in their own image. The tragedy, however, as Wilde so perceptively noted, was that these Western images almost totally ignored the real Japan.

American imagery of Japan between 1853 and Pearl Harbor swung from positive highs to negative lows in rapid succession. Initial condescending images were rapidly displaced by feelings of admiration and wonder which were then again replaced by feelings of hostility and fear that led directly to Pearl Harbor. It is probable that a more realistic view of Japan might have avoided much of the tension between the two nations throughout their relationship.

Ideas and images of another culture are not often faithful representations of the culture that they describe. On the contrary, they often tell us more about ourselves than they do about the culture being investigated. The American image of China since the mid-nineteenth century has shifted violently from one of positive fascination to great enmity. In recent decades the view of China moved from one of a heroic nation and ally

---

[12] Ibid.

[13] Patrick Smith, *Japan: A Reinterpretation* (New York: Vintage Books, 1997), pp. 3-4.

fighting Japanese aggression to that of a pariah state, a deceitful supporter of international communism and enemy of the American way of life and, in the 1990s, a competitive partner which in late 2001 strongly supported the American war against terrorism. Thus, understanding a culture's views of another society can be useful for the social historian wishing to analyze contemporary attitudes within his own culture.

Americans knew virtually nothing about East Asia when Perry's expedition set sail in the early 1850s. The shelf list at the Widener Library at Harvard University recorded only sixteen items published about Japan, China or Korea prior to 1840.[14] This means that for a long time "East Asia was an esoteric subject. Absorbed in domestic political, social and economic issues of the first importance, very few Americans knew, and almost no one cared about East Asia. There was virtually no informed opinion about East Asia in colonial and revolutionary America. People knew that the region existed, that it produced luxury goods like silk and chinaware, and that it was the source of much of the tea that they drank. They identified Asia as a place of antiquity, mystery, splendor and riches.[15] It was only after 1784 when American merchants began trading with China that the new nation got its first real glimpse at Asia. American relationships with China during the early nineteenth century since Americans were as yet not terribly interested in any form of imperialist expansion. "This limited role had compensatory advantages for both Americans and Chinese:

> [T]he nearly complete absence of the American government from the scene improved the environment for an economic relationship based upon the mutually beneficial exchange of goods. It

---

[14] John C. Perry, James C. Thompson and Peter W. Stanley, *Sentimental Imperialists: The American Experience in East Asia* (New York: Harper and Row, 1981), p. 6

[15] Ibid.

was credible, in this light, that commercial relations between the United States and China might contribute to the improvement and elevation of peoples on both sides of the Pacific and might ultimately forge a new harmony of races and interests. This gave high ethical sanction to what might otherwise have seemed merely a matter of balancing payments and scrounging profits.[16]

The nearly century and a half relationship between the United States and Japan has shifted between periods of enmity and amity. American popular perceptions of Japanese have shifted according to the state of relations between the two powers. Since Pearl Harbor Americans have thought of Japanese alternatively as being truly kind or warlike and cruel, artistic and charming, business-oriented and clever, and at times even deceitful. These perceptions are both stereotypical and one-dimensional and reveal more about the thinking of the observer than the observed.

Sociologists have remarked that the wildly divergent perceptions that Americans have held about Japan reveals the true shallow nature of these attitudes. They note that most Americans do not think much about Japan at all which means that their impressions are likely to be both hasty and contradictory. Because so few Americans understand Japanese national character, it is easier to form speculative stereotypes whose foundations are so weak that they shift with even the slightest alteration in Japan's relationship with the United States. Furthermore, even though there are many reputable Japanologists in North America writing and teaching about Japan, most popular images of the Japanese stem from the vernacular press and romantic novels such as *Shogun*, the authors of which have little appreciation for the intricacies of Japanese culture.

Clearly, if a writer approaches a subject with a strong preconceived image, his or her finished work at best will show a highly blemished view of reality. But if the work is widely read and discussed, an unsuspecting

---

[16] Ibid, p. 13.

public might accept the author's views as gospel truth. These views in turn can influence foreign policy decisions and influence views that policymakers have of that culture. Pearl Buck and her celebrated but badly flawed novel, *The Good Earth,* certainly helped to frame a false image of China during the 1930s. But just as Buck's work helped frame American policies in the 1930s, Americans who wrote and lectured about Meiji Japan also played an important role in shaping popular images of the Japanese.

The first Americans to visit Japan in the 1850s and 1860s were a motley crew of sailors, traders, diplomats and adventurers. Because few of these gentlemen were well-educated and had any skill or interest in writing, their contributions to American understanding of Japan were few. It was not until the early 1870s, when the new Meiji government began to hire a large number highly educated Americans and Europeans as advisors, that Americans began to get some picture of Japan in the form of letters, articles and books.

The first-generation of American visitors to Japan, however, had no background training in the nation's culture and produced work of little distinction. But their comments in the vernacular press did rouse the curiosity of many Americans. Throughout the 1870s there began a flood of Americans visiting Japan including engineers and traders, sightseers and doctors, art collectors and linguists. Many of these instant "experts" on Japan produced travelogues that described their arrival in Yokohama, their trips to the "Dieboots" (Daibutsu; "Great Buddha") in Kamakura and the great shrines and temples in Kyoto and Nikko, other trips into the interior, and a few cursory comments on "quaint" Japanese customs. Basil Chamberlain, a long time Meiji-era resident of Japan, lamented in his own distinctive work, *Things Japanese*, that none of these writers had contributed a perceptive view of the "real" Japan.

Chamberlain, however, was not entirely correct. William Elliot Griffis (1840-1928), the first authentic American Japanologist, wrote a stream of articles and books about Japan from his arrival in Fukui as a teacher in 1869 until his death in 1928. His 1890 work, *The Mikado's Empire,* became the most widely read book on Japan a century ago and remains a classic. Zoologist Edward Sylvester Morse's *Japan Day by Day* was another skillfully written and widely read tome. But their scholarly and well-informed views were the rare exception.

Writer and journalist Lafcadio Hearn (1850-1904) had an immense following in the United States during his fourteen-year residence in Japan which began in 1890. Hearn's views of traditional Japan are very well informed, but he had a deep disdain for their rapid modernization process which inevitably meant a move away from the traditional Japanese values which he romanticized in much of his writing. Hearn's sentimental interpretations of "old" Japan colored the views of many Western readers some of whom got the false image that Japan was little more than a quaint "Madame Butterfly" nation. They were thus shocked when the Japanese military crushed first China and then supposedly mighty Russia in successive wars in 1894-95 and 1904-05.

THE CHANGING IMAGERY OF JAPAN

There are three distinct model images of Japan presented by American writers between Commodore Perry's first visit in 1853 and the end of World War II in 1945. The first phase, which began with published reports by Perry and other observers and which lingered into the early 1870s, depicted a backward, sometimes "barbarian" and pagan Japan that badly required America's guidance and tutelage to help it join the "civilized" world. The second phase, which extended from the mid-1870s until Japan's 1905 victory over Russia, is an emphatic reversal of the earlier image. While some writers became fixated with seeming exotic portraits of Japanese society, others marveled at Japan's rapid Westernization. They saw in Japan a superb example of how non-Western nations could benefit from the combined effects of science and Christianity. This romantic image changed abruptly during the first decade of the twentieth century when Japan emerged as a modern power in direct competition with the Western imperialist nations for economic and political control of Asia. Japan and its people were then portrayed in very sinister tones as "cunning and untrustworthy" beings, the "yellow peril" that sought to destroy Western civilization. This phase continued through Japan's humiliating defeat in 1945 when Americans, now occupying a humbled Japan, once again began to perceive the Japanese in a more favorable light.

The First Phase: Commodore Perry saw the United States as the herald of the "civilized world" whose humanitarian mission" was to guide Japan away from its primitive state. Perry depicted Japanese as "sagacious" and "deceitful" people who had little understanding of "honor" and other aspects of a civilized society. Clark wrote:

> You can scarcely imagine the impressions of one fresh from a Christian land at the first view of the heathenism of which we had heard, but never seen. There is no more Sabbath here than if the Ten Commandments were never written. The sounds of labor are heard in every direction and sin and corruption abound in their worst forms. Instead of church bells, I hear ever and anon the deep prolonged sound of the great bell of the heathen temple as it strikes to announce that another soul has entered to bow down to the idol. Instead of sacred music, I hear fire crackers in an adjacent burying ground, where worship is going on to the spirits of the dead.

> Clark later wrote that "[T]rue progress depends more upon the development of sound principles within the heart of the nation, than it does upon costly importation of material appliances from without."[17]

---

[17] Quoted in Henning, p. 74.

W. E. Griffis' first impressions in the early 1870s were just as haughty and condescending. Japan historian Thom Burns writes about Griffis' early published views of Japan:[18]

> Griffis ends his book by asking, "Can an Asian despotism, based on paganism, regenerate itself?…Can a nation appropriate the fruits of Christian civilization without its roots? I believe not." Without Christianity "the enlightened ideas of government and law" and "the rights of the individual," Japan will gain little more than a "glittering veneer of material civilization" which "in the presence of superior Aggressive nations of the West," will cause "Dai Nippon" to "fall like the doomed races of America."

Both Clark and Griffis had analyzed the peculiarities and mysteries of Japan and had lived in its modern cities as well as its impoverished countryside. America's part in bringing Japan to the civilized world meant teaching it the peculiarities of science, democracy and Christianity. These were, after all, the elements the United States had at its birth.

The Romantic Phase (1870s-early 1900s) The romantic phase of American perceptions of Japan dominated the last decades of the nineteenth century. This stage cast Japan in a very different light than before.

The ignorant pigmy pagans of Japan had flabbergasted their Western guests with their ability to modernize quickly. The first railroad connecting Tokyo and Yokohama was up and running as early as 1871 and telegraph wires were found everywhere. The students that Clark, Griffis and others encountered were diligent, courteous, and quick learners. Clark praises them for their ability to devour and comprehend a difficult scientific textbook at least as fast as their American counterparts. Their politeness, obvious morality, and dedication to both thrift and hard work parallel the Puritan work ethic espoused by many contemporary American writers.

---

[18] Burns, p. 29.

The Japanese were surely exhibiting the best traits of the United States and would become in rapid order the foundation stone for the implantation of "Anglo-Saxon" civilization in East Asia. America must therefore support and nurture its apt pupil Japan. The fact that Japan had not as yet become a Christian nation was not a cause for concern. Japan was by then "latently" a Christian nation because it displayed all of the qualities (morality, thrift, modernization etc) of a good Christian nation. True conversion to Christianity would come in due course.

One finds these ideas in the writings of both Griffis and Clark, who were both scientists and theologians. Both Griffis and Clark shared a strong faith in the inevitable benefits of science, God and progress. Their observations of Japan's rapid modernization made them strong advocates of the belief that Japan represented the best chance for the spread of "Anglo-Saxon civilization" to the East. They admired Japan not only because it had developed Western science and technology, but also because the Japanese were also laying the foundations for universal education and democracy and Christian ethics.

The "Japan as Enemy" Phase (early 1900s-1945): The romantic pro-Japanese views of Japan began to change rapidly at the start of the twentieth century. Strong support for Japan in the Russo-Japanese War marks the high point of American appreciation for Japan., However, Japan's emergence as a major imperialist power after the war that could threaten American interests in the Pacific brought angry and very negative representations of Japan in the American media. The stage was set for nearly four decades of harsh confrontations over a wide range of issues including immigration, power, prestige and imperialism that resulted in the Pearl Harbor and the Pacific War.

These rapid positive-then-negative shift in American thinking about Japan continued after the war as well. When Japan behaved once again in the late 1940s and 1950s as our dutiful student and junior partner, the image of Tokyo was very good. Later, in the 1980s when Japan again became a major competitor and therefore a threat to the United States,

Japan was once again portrayed as the enemy. One memory that shall remain glued in the minds of many Americans is the image of Republican Congressmen destroying Japanese-made appliances on the steps of the Capitol in the mid-1980s. But by the late 1990s, however, when a recession-plagued Japan no longer seemed to threaten an increasingly prosperous America, the negative image of Japan had dissipated. After the terrorist acts of 11 September 2001, the United States began to actively seek Japanese military assistance in the Middle East.

The Role of Edward Warren Clark as an Image Maker

The purpose of this research is to study the writings of one early American image-maker in Japan, Edward Warren Clark. Clark, who resided in Japan from 1871-75 and who later returned for extensive visits in 1895 and 1904, wrote and lectured frequently about Japan. Clark wrote three books: *Life and Adventure in Japan* Ä (New York: American Tract Society,1878), *From Hong Kong to the Himalayas or, Three Thousand Miles Through Asia to India* (New York: American Tract Society, 1881), and *Katz Awa, the "Bismarck of Japan" or the Story of a Noble Life* (New York: B. F. Buck and Co., 1904).

Clark also wrote articles in at least nine newspapers and two journals. The newspapers included: *The New York Evening Post, The Brooklyn Daily Argus, The New York Daily Tribune* and the *Albany Evening Journal*. The *Post*, which is still published in New York, and the *Tribune*, were leading newspapers of the period. Clark also wrote articles in the *International Review* and *The Far West*. Clark's 1872 lecture on Euclidean geometry was translated into Japanese by two of his students and was an important text on the subject for many years in Japan. The American Tract Society, a well-known publisher of books on missionary subjects, published many copies of his first two books and circulated them widely. Clark also wrote extensively for several well-known American newspapers and journals and kept in touch with his Griffis, his closest friend.

What makes Clark a fascinating model for research is the evolution of his thinking about Japan which clearly parallels and represents what many late nineteenth century writers, especially "Christian" authors, were writing about Japan. Clark went to Japan in 1871 with a rather haughty air of superiority that he, the representative of the most progressive and advanced civilized nation on earth, would bring the blessings of Christianity and modern times to the backward and pagan peoples of Japan. Soon after his arrival in Japan, however, he began what became a lifelong fascination and admiration for Japan which mirrored sentiments in the American press in the 1870s and 1880s.

Late in life Clark became convinced that Japan was in fact a latently Christian nation that stood the best chance of both adopting and spreading the blessings of Anglo-Saxon civilization to Asia. Clark's very active support for Japan's war effort during the Russo-Japanese War (1904-05) very accurately reflect pro-Japanese American sentiment that Japan was the force for progress while Russia symbolized all that was backward and regressive. There are thus strong parallels between the thinking and writing and prevailing sentiments of many Americans during Clark's period of scholarly activity. It is thus through Clark that we can perhaps get a good view of American sentiments towards Japan during the Meiji period.

Clark's Life and Background

Clark, who became an Episcopal priest in the United States following his return from Japan, came from a very religious family. His father, Rufus W. Clark, was also an Episcopal priest, and he had an uncle who became the Episcopal bishop of Rhode Island.[19]

---

[19] For the best biographical sketch of Clark's life, see Iida Hiroshi, *E. W. Kurakucho 'Nihon ni okeru Seikatsu to Keiken' (E. W. Clark's Life and Adventure in Japan)* Shizuoka-ken Eigagukushi Shiryo (Materials on the History of English Studies in Shizuoka Prefecture) (shizuoka, 1955.

See also: Yamamoto Yukinori, *Shizuoka Han to Oyatoi Gaikokujin Kyoshi: E . Kuraku)* (Shizuoka Han and the Foreign Hired Teacher: E. W. Clark) in Doshisha Daigaku Jinbun Kagaku Kenkyujo, Kiristukyo Shakai Mondai Kenkyu, Vol. 29 (1981).

Ministers, like career soldiers and college professors, move frequently during their careers and the Clark family was no exception. E. Warren Clark was born in Portsmouth, New Hampshire, and spent his boyhood in places like East Boston, Massachusetts and in Brooklyn and Albany, New York before going to college.

Clark entered Rutgers University in New Jersey in the fall of 1867 and graduated in 1869 with majors in Chemistry and Physics. He began a life-long friendship there with a fellow student, W.E. Griffis. He also met a number of Japanese students who were studying at Rutgers. They included the two sons of Iwakura Tomomi (1825-83), a leading statesman in the Meiji government, and the son of Katsu Kaishu (Rintaro, 1826-99), a leading Meiji era politician and confidant of the former Tokugawa shogun. Hatakeyama Yoshinari, who later became Director of the Kaisei Gakko (later Tokyo Imperial University) was another of Clark's friends. These friendships would later be invaluable to Clark during his years in Japan.

After his graduation in 1869, Clark, having decided upon a career in the ministry, departed for a brief study in Geneva, Switzerland. Meanwhile, his friend Griffis had left for Japan to accept a teaching position in the city of Fukui, then the capital of Echizen Province (now Fukui Prefecture). The governor (daimyo) of Echizen wanted to build a base for Western learning in his province and had asked Guido F. Verbeck, a teacher living in Tokyo who played an instrumental role in creating the Kaisei Gakko. Verbeck strongly recommended Griffis who immediately accepted the position and left for Japan in 1870.

Soon after Griffis arrived in Japan, he received a letter from Katsu Kaishu requesting his recommendation of a teacher for the newly founded Gakumonjo, a school for Western studies which the Tokugawa family had opened in late 1868 in Shizuoka soon after the Tokugawa Shogunate had collapsed and the Tokugawa family was forced into domestic exile at its ancestral base.[20] Clark received an invitation to teach at the Shizuoka school and rapidly made his way to Tokyo to take up the post. After signing his contract in Tokyo, he made the then rather arduous journey overland to Shizuoka.

Clark taught at the Gakumonjo from 1871 to 1873 and then accepted an invitation to move to Tokyo to teach at the Kaisei Gakko where he helped to found what is now the Chemistry Department at Tokyo University. Clark left Japan in 1875 and returned to the United States via China, India, and Europe. He studied for the Episcopal ministry in Philadelphia and became a priest in 1879. He married in 1879 and fathered eight children. He served in several parishes in upstate New York, the Midwest and Florida before dying from tuberculosis in 1907. Clark also formed a travel company that took him on three global tours in his latter years including the 1904 visit to Japan.

The goal of this work is to provide the reader with a unique view of Japanese-American relations before the two nations advanced along the path that led to Pearl Harbor. This chapter will enhance the student's understanding of a dynamic relationship that continues to challenge policy-makers today.

---

[20] One reason that the Tokugawa family sponsored the school was to educate young (samurai) men in the family and region so that the Tokugawa's might regain power and influence in the new government. The school used Clark in a rather interesting manner. Clark would lecture about science to a group of perhaps 20-25 older student tutors who understood English in the morning and in the afternoon each tutor would repeat the same lecture and laboratory demonstrations to groups of younger students. Many graduates of the school themselves went on to become teachers in schools across Japan. This methodology allowed the rapid dissemination of "Western knowledge" across Japan.

SECOND INTRODUCTION

E. WARREN CLARK: A YANKEE IN MEIJI JAPAN:

By Jessica D. Puglisi
Mary Baldwin College

Before reading *Life and Adventure in Japan*, the reader should realize that one is entering into much more than just an engrossing account of a visit to Japan by a young American scientist and teacher. The author is an astute observer who gives us a unique glimpse both into 19th century Japanese and American culture, relying on his own life experiences as a means of comparison with what he en-counters in Japan. As he relays the intricacies of his attempts to teach the "pagans" about Christianity as well as science, Clark reveals the patterns of his own growth and evolution of thought in such a way that his work chronicles the author's personal growth in tandem with his experiences.

E. Warren Clark begins his evolutional journey as an 1869 graduate of Rutgers College, traveling to Japan in 1871 through a program that brought recent college graduates in to teach at Japanese universities for three-year stints. Upon his arrival in Japan, he demonstrates a deep-seated patriotism and love for the United States, which at times, runs almost to the point of arrogance or ethno-centrism. Although it is refreshing in today's world where so many Americans express frequent criticism for their country and government to read an account of a young man with such a strong sense of nationalism, Clark initially runs a risk of being so closed-minded in his convictions of the United States' superiority to Japan as to miss the lessons that the Japanese have to teach him. His comparisons of the Japanese way of life to his own have a tendency to leave the former falling short. This gives the reader an intriguing peek into the minds of Victorian-era Americans; if Clark can be considered a standard for other well-educated young men during this time, we find that God and country (in that order) are just as important to Americans in the 1870s as in the days of the earliest New England settlers as well as for flag wavers today particularly after the September 11 terrorist incident.

The author's continuous attempts to bring Christianity to the "heathen masses" are demonstrative of a continuance of Puritan-like views that seem to have remained through 1878, and can even be found to be held by Clark, who, as a recent college graduate, can be expected to be more liberal than most. At times, it may almost seem to the reader as though his primary purpose in coming to Japan is one of missionary work rather than that of serving as a scientific and technological resource to the Japanese. Much of Clark's account is devoted to the time and effort he commits to running Sunday school classes and Bible studies with the aim of converting the Japanese people as well as instilling Christian values and ideals into their population. Ironically however, it is these same Christian values, which Clark believes need to be instilled in the Japanese, that ultimately contribute to his growing respect for them; for although they do not call themselves Christians, the author finds the Japanese to personify many Christian values[21] through their everyday character and conduct, and perhaps, at times, even more so than many of those in the U.S. identifying themselves as Christian.

Clark demonstrates early in the book that he finds the Japanese lack of technical knowledge and experience only slightly less appalling than the

---

[21] Clark in various letters later in his career calls the Japanese "latent" Christians.

condition of their immortal souls. On at least two occasions, he relays tales of the Japanese amazement at his scientific experiments, even describing his attempts and sometime successes at embarrassing Japanese officials who are too "dignified" to participate in his demonstrations. His amusement at their ignorance of technology soon fades to respect however, as he begins to recognize their cultural capacity and love for learning. After describing the Japanese students as more adapt at learning than any other students he has encountered, even in the United States, Clark is further impressed when, during the construction of his house, the Japanese carpenters are able to produce perfect replicas of the furniture he desires, solely from his descriptions. Clark is continually amazed, learning that what the Japanese people lack in scientific advancement and technology, they make up for in efficiency and artfulness. He is, for example, fascinated with the bright tattoos covering the backs of the coolies carrying his *kango*[22] and their uncanny knack of pacing themselves so that they show no signs of fatigue even after a full day of travel. These and other numerous lively details Clark gives of the sights, sounds, food, and culture during his stay, serve as a virtual snapshot of Japan at this era, well before much modernization has taken place.

The accounts of the author's interactions with the Japanese people are particularly descriptive, giving the reader a clear, historically accurate image of what everyday life must have been like in Japan in the 1870s. Clark writes of everyone and everything he sees, from the "Tycoon" (Shogun) to the merest peasant; and the result is a well-splayed image including Japanese of every walk of life. The verbal caricatures he uses to depict each man, woman, and child cause the reader to smile as he or she conjures the menagerie of people Clark encounters. In addition to being educational and informative, each of the author's interactions with the people of Japan also contribute to his personal metamorphosis in such a

---

[22] A kind of portable sedan chair with a roof designed for the transport of dignitaries.

way that Clark's transition of thought is entirely complete as he begins his journey back across the Pacific Ocean to the United States.

As he prepares to return to his home in the US in 1875, Clark's descriptions lose the element of comparison to the Western culture to which he is used, and take on a sort of awe filled reverence, as well as a sense of what will be missed. He has come to respect the Japanese so much that he can at least comprehend the reasoning behind the argument for keeping Christianity out of Japan. This understanding, coupled with Clark's own acknowledgement of the Imperial Mint to be comparable, if not superior to the U.S. Mint in Pennsylvania, highlights Clark's transformation more so than any other point in the work. Arguably, some of the sense of dread Clark experiences as he leaves Japan, can be attributed to his now growing sense of the advantages of, as well as a sense of what can be gained through imitating some aspects of Japanese culture.

Like the notches Clark, comparing himself to Robinson Crusoe, makes in sticks to aid himself in measuring the passing of days, weeks, and months, E. Warren Clark's *Life and Adventure in Japan* is an excellent gauge of one man's transition to cultural acceptance and understanding, and ultimately, to what one might call his enlightenment.

Chapter 1

First Sight of Japan

At early dawn on Wednesday, October 25th, I looked out of my stateroom window from the steamer Great Republic, and lo! The snow white dome of the Fuji-Yama, the "Matchless Mountain" of Japan, rising like a temple of beauty above the clouds and mist; and as I caught sight of it the sun rose higher and higher, causing the mountain to brighten up, and its face to smile a welcome to us in our approach to the old, old world.

Slowly we steamed up the great bay of Yedo,[23] passing the verdure-covered cliffs, rocky promontories, and small islets clothed in brightest green,

---

[23] Edo (now Tokyo) Harbor.

while here and there the thatched-roof cottages of the fishermen were scattered along the shore.

A slight breeze rippled the surface of the water, and Japanese junks came scudding by under full sail. The junks had low prows and very high sterns, with broad sails sometimes made of matting or bamboo, and having large characters inscribed on black bands of cloth, with which the mainsail was ornamented. The cargo of the junk was carried amidship, with a bamboo roof built over it; and not a particle of paint appeared on the whole craft. The junks came quite near the steamer, dashing the spray from their low prows, and rocking violently in the rollers left in the wake of the Great Republic

With the Captain's permission, I brought my new flag on deck, presented my friends far away, and up went my bright star-spangled banner in place of the ship's dilapidated ensign, and it flapped and fluttered proudly from the stern of the steamer.

As we passed vessel after vessel of various nationalities lying at anchor in the harbor, *that* flag was saluted with respect—German, Italian, English, French, Dutch, and other ships dipped their colors as we went by, and only ceased when the signal-gun from our steamer announced that we had made fast to our moorings in Yokohama Bay.

Swarms of little skiffs surrounded us, sculled by nearly naked Japanese, with brawny arms and brown skins. Dropping into one of these boats, I made for the shore. Alone I wandered off, and peculiar were my feelings as I wended my way among the strange sights and people.

It is said that the *sounds* of a place first attract the stranger's attention, and so it was here. I heard an unearthly shout or yell, repeated in quick and regular succession, and turning down the street I saw a line of rough wooden carts drawn by strong coolies, who tugged away like horses and gave guttural yells in keeping step with each other.

Boxes of tea were piled on the carts, and as I passed by the stone houses on a side street I could smell the sweet aroma of the tea that was being "refired" within, and hear the merry prattle in a strange tongue of the tea-girls as they sang together and stirred the tea leaves on the hot copper ovens.

Taking a straight street to the left, I passed through a portion of the foreign settlement, which was substantial and comfortable, and came to a bridge crossing the canal. On ascending a steep flight of steps, I reached the top of "The Bluff," where many English and Americans live; from this point, a beautiful view spread before me of the bay, shipping, city, and the native town of Yokohama.

I met many kind friends at the American Mission Home, a beautiful building on "The Bluff," where Japanese girls are instructed in Christian truth, and where the first Sunday school in Japan was established.

After a few days, the Japanese officials arrived at Yokohama who were appointed to conduct me to their distant province in the interior of the country.

I had engaged to go the city of Shidz-u-o-ka, one hundred miles southwest of To-kio, to take charge of a scientific school there, and teach the Japanese in chemistry, physics, and other branches of study. I was to be liberally paid by the Japanese Government, who were also to furnish my horses, guards, interpreters, philosophical apparatus, attendants, and give me a large temple in which to live. Thirteen long articles, written in Chinese, Japanese, and English, and forming three imposing-looking books, constituted the "contract" or agreement made between us for the space of three years.

But when I came to sign the agreement, I found that the "Dai-jo-kan"—as the Council of State is called—had slyly inserted a clause forbidding me to teach Christianity, and binding me to silence on all religious subjects for a space of three years. Many reasons prompted me to accept, and some of my friends urged me to sign the contract as it was. The interpreter said, "Sign the promise; but when you get way off in the country you can break it and teach what you please." Others said, "Sign it or you will lose $300 a month, and all your good chances besides; some mere adventurer may get the position, who will do the people more harm than you can do them good."

It was a great dilemma, for I had spent all my money in coming to Japan and getting ready to go into the interior, and were the contract to fail I should find myself in a tight place.

Nevertheless, I determined to stand firm on the principle at stake, and sent word to the government that unless the objectionable clause was withdrawn, the contract could not be accepted. "It is impossible," I added, "for a Christian to dwell three years in the midst of a pagan people, and yet keep entire silence on the subject nearest his heart."

To my surprise an answer was returned after three days saying that the clause against Christianity should be stricken out; and the messenger who brought me the news exclaimed, "You have conquered, and have broken down a strong Japanese wall. Now you can also teach us the Bible and Christianity!"

I mention this to show that it pays to hold fast to the right, at whatever apparent cost; for, instead of thinking less of me, or being vexed at my obstinacy, the Japanese officials were more friendly that ever, and respected the "pluck" displayed.

They immediately advanced all the necessary funds to meet the heavy expenses incurred, and were so liberal and polite as to excite my gratitude and astonishment. Under their kindly assistance, I was soon ready to start on the long journey.

But never before had I so many things to think of at once. Not only had I the care of perfecting my official arrangements, but I had all the minute details of "first going to housekeeping" beyond the range of civilization.

Imagine yourself going to keep house where a real house was never known! Imagine yourself endeavoring to furnish said houses where furniture was never heard of; where bedsteads and beds and carpets and stoves were never seen; where mirrors and chimneys and coal had not even been dreamed of. Imagine yourself going to live a certain number of years in said house and place. The probability is you would want something to eat during your sojourn; but there beef-steaks and mutton-chops are unknown, a loaf of bread is a myth, and milk, butter, and cheese are fairy tales.

Perhaps now and then you would like to know the time of day. But no town-clock ever strikes to inform you, no chronometer exists by which to set your watch when it stops, no almanac to tell the day of the week or the month when you have forgotten them. In fact, I frequently *did* forget the day of the week, and once kept the scientific school waiting several hours for me, supposing it was Sunday! After that I thought of cutting notches in a stick every day, after Robinson Crusoe's fashion; and when my watch stopped I would set it by the sun-dial, which I made with two sticks, a compass, and a string.

Na-ka-mu-ra was the name of one of the officers sent from the province where I was going; and although he was the most noted scholar of Chinese literature in Japan, he was simple as a child, and quite amusing in his use of broken English. He called at the Mission Home to see me one day, while I was off making some purchases, and, as he awaited my return, the children of the Home volunteered to entertain him. "They take out several cards," he wrote, "singing the songs which are written on them" (Sunday-school hymns), "then, passing the biblical pictures, very fine, to me, they said, 'While you look at them Mr. Clark will soon be returned.' The girls again merrily explained them to me, saying, 'This is John the Baptist,' This is dove,' 'This is Jesus,' 'This is Abraham sacrificing his son,' and the like. During one hour I feel myself to get some advantages from the surrounding children."

Not long after this Nakamura boldly presented a memorial to the imperial government suggesting that they build a Christian church in Tokyo! in order that Japanese subjects might have an opportunity of being instructed in the truth. Of course, the government did not quite see it in that light. Nakumura was appointed to go abroad with the Japanese embassy then starting for America, but he declined, saying that he had once lived in a Christian country—England—without learning

Christianity, and now he wished to retire to his own province and study religious subjects with his foreign teacher. He was subsequently my warmest friend and most intimate companion; he became a devout Christian under the instruction of my Bible-class, and frequently he would sign himself, "your most humble servant, and to be your future and forever friend in the spiritual world."

On my last Sabbath in Yokohama I attended the little chapel where foreigners are accustomed to assemble, and listened to an interesting sermon from Rev. Mr. H—, a missionary of North China. It was a communion service, my first in Japan, and the last that I should have for a long, long time, as I was going where there were no Christians. On returning from church I wrote home, saying:

"The more I enjoyed the service, the more vividly it brought upon me the realization of the keen deprivation I am to suffer in being cut off from all holy associations, and how I shall long for the strength gained from Christian sympathy and the sound of the Gospel.

"You can scarcely imagine the impressions of one fresh from a Christian land at the first view of the heathenism of which he had never heard but never seen. There is no more Sabbath here than if the Ten Commandments were never written. The sounds of labor are heard in every direction, and sin and corruption abound in their worst forms. Instead of church bells, I hear ever and anon the deep, prolonged sound of the great bell of the heathen temple, as it strikes to announce that another soul has entered to bow down to the idol. Instead of sacred music, I hear firecrackers in an adjacent Chinese burying-ground, where worship is going on to the spirits of the dead. As I visited the temples of Yedo the other day, and saw the hundreds of human beings prostrated before their images and calling upon their gods, it did seem to me the most pitiable sight I ever witnessed; and as I moved among the millions in the great capital of Japan who never heard the name of Christ, it seemed to be too solemn to be true. Possibly I may become so accustomed to heathenism and its accompaniments as not to feel their painful reality, but I trust I may never lose the earnest desire to turn these poor deluded souls from their errors."

On the following Monday the horses and guards appeared at the door, and as my furniture and freight had been sent by sea on a Japanese junk, I bade farewell to all my new-made friends at Yokohama, and started off with the guards to encounter the strange experiences and adventures of life in the heart of Japan.

Chapter 2

A Journey on the "Tokaido"

The great public thoroughfare of Japan is called the "To-kai-do." It is several hundred miles in length, and passes along the seashore and over the mountains, connecting the ancient capital, Kyoto, near Lake Biwa, with the modern capital, Tokyo, at the head of Yedo Bay.

The road is flanked on either side with venerable pines, which have shaded generations of travelers and pilgrims who have passed to and fro through this beautiful country. Near the seashore, it is protected by earthen embankments, and over the steep declivities of the mountains, it is paved with stones. It runs through innumerable villages and towns, and its wayside is the best possible place to study the country life and character of the people.

Here you may meet the two-sworded "Samurai," as the military gentlemen are called who wear long, sharp swords thrust in their belts, and who sometimes look very fiercely at foreigners, whom they do not love overmuch for invading the sacred seclusion of their country. Here you meet the farmers also, carrying their produce to market, and the coolies, trudging along with their burdens suspended from the ends of a pole carried on the shoulder.

Here you meet bands of pilgrims clothed in white, wearing broad bamboo hats, and carrying as small bell in one hand and a long staff in the other. On the staff were strips of paper prayers, and the little bells tinkled continually to call the attention of the gods to the prayers while the pilgrims were on their journey to the various heathen shrines.

The country people were very polite and, as we passed them on the road each one would bow and exclaim, "Ohayoo! (Good morning). The children would also nod their little heads politely, and touch their foreheads as a mark of respect.

In passing through one of the towns on the "Tokaido" we saw a long ladder standing upright at the side of the street, upon which a man climbed whenever the fire alarm sounded. The houses were simply wooden shanties, with paper sliding doors, and when they caught fire, as they frequently did, the man on the ladder would shout to his neighbors, and they would run together and pull down the house, instead of attempting to extinguish the flames.

On the roadside a stream of water is seen, which the natives use in cooking and washing. The open space in front of each house is used for drying fish, sifting grain, and also for sunning the babies and children who swarm by the roadside, and who use this space frequently for a playground.

The mountain Fuji-Yama is seen in the distance.

We turned aside a few miles to visit "Dai-Butz," the great bronze idol of Japan,[24] which is about fifty feet in height. It stands near the former site of

---

[24] The Daibutsu (great Buddha) is located in Kamakura, today an hour by train from Tokyo.

the great historic interest, but which passed away some centuries ago, leaving scarcely a vestige behind, except this idol and a large temple.

The colossal image represents Buddha sitting in a lotus-lily, in the state called "nirvana," which is a kind of divine sleep or unconsciousness. This is the heavenly state, which the devout Buddhist hopes to attain. Not a heaven of holy activity and of joyous worship, but a *sleep* of eternal unconsciousness, an absorption into Buddha! Yet, there is certainly something very peaceful and even beautiful in the expression of repose on that bronze face, and I do not wonder that multitudes of the ignorant pilgrims worship it with awe.

In front of the image are two vases containing large bronze lotus-lilies with expanding leaves, and between the vases is a bronze brazier where incense may be burnt. Dai-Butz I very imposing without, but he is entirely empty within; for you may go inside of him, by passing through a small door, and find his hollow form lined with shelves, on which small gilt idols are ranged. His ears are very large, as all ears are on all idols, and his massive head is covered with concentric rows of snail-shells, which gathered there to protect his sacred person from the sun when in mythological times he rose from the sea.

After studying the image as a work of art, I climbed up into his capacious lap, and sat upon one of his thumbs, which were placed together in a devout attitude. Here I began to sing the long-meter doxology, to the astonishment of the priest standing below, who could not understand the words, and wondered what the matter was! A year after this I sang the same hymn in Dai-Butz's lap, with half a dozen other people; and we told the priest we were praising the true God, that the time was at hand when idolatry in Japan was going down, never to rise again, and that even Dai-Butz would no longer be worshipped.

Not far from this great image is the beautiful island of In-o-shi-ma,[25] close by the shore, where shrines and temples are found embowered

---

[25] Enoshima, a small mountainous island connected to Kamakura by a bridge.

among the trees high up on the rocky cliffs, and where you may descend to submarine caverns, to reach which I had to swim around the rocks and allow myself to be swept into a dark and dreary cavern by the waves. Here a naked priest stood by a stone altar. On the ledges of the rock, where the surf rolled and dashed high in the air, little Japanese urchins were diving for pennies in the deep green water, protected by the grottos formed at the foot of the cliff; they would catch a penny when thrown into the water long before it reached the bottom.

We spent the first night at a large city on the Tokaido, and the next morning found us galloping along the level road leading toward O-da-wa-ra, a city at the foot of the Ha-ko-ne mountain pass. The whole journey to Shidz-u-o-ka required five days, for you must remember there were no steam-cars, coaches, or modern conveniences of travel. Besides, I very soon found that it was to be a journey of Japanese etiquette the whole way. As we approached the province where I was to live, whole villages appeared specially prepared for my reception. The native officials would come out to meet us, dressed in flowing robes, and salute me in the way they used to receive the Dai-mios,[26] or distinguished princes, in olden times. Although they were two-sworded men of rank, they would kneel in front of our horses and bow their heads to the earth, heaving a deep sign of respect that sounded like a miniature typhoon!

These Yaconims, or officials, would escort us on foot through the whole length of the district under their jurisdiction, picking up any stray straw or stone that happened in the way, and motioning all carts and traffic to the side of the road with a wave of authority that made all plebeians drop on their knees at once, and keep there until our august presence was passed.

It tickled my Yankee glee not a little to touch up the horses now and then, causing these sedate officials to perform feats of pedestrianism such as they had scarcely before been attempted. They took it in good part, and I usually favored them with an extra "smile" for their pains. If I started on

---

[26] Daimyo or provincial lords/governors

a brisk trot, however, and shouted, "Sayonara!" (Goodbye), they would fall at once on their faces, keeping their heads bowed between their hands until we had disappeared from view.

At the next village we would have to go through the very same formalities, until, after a dozen or more were passed, it became rather monotonous. Whole neighborhoods were thrown into agitation by the arrival in their midst of such a strange-looking creature as the "foreigner," and I was evidently as great a curiosity to the people as they were to me. Long lines of awestruck faces presented themselves at every window and door and crevice, and crowds of women and children thronged the narrow lanes as we galloped through the principal street, making the old town echo with the clatter of our horses' feet.

On crossing the Hakone range of mountains, it became necessary to change our horses for peculiar vehicles called "kan-gos," carried on men's shoulders. The "kan-go" is like a broad cane chair without legs, slung securely on a thick pole, and in which you must squat, with the happy alternative of breaking your neck above or twisting your legs out of joint below. How to get into it was a mystery, so I just gave a pitch and tumble, leaving it to chance whether I came in right side up or not.

When I was fairly stowed away in the kango, two naked coolies raised it from the ground and placed the ends of the pole on their brawny shoulders. Off they trudged, as though I were simply a bag of rice, or a box of cheese, and, jolting me up and down like a bowlful of jelly, they slowly climbed the steep and stone-paved path of the mountains. Now and then, they rested the ends of the pole upon their stout bamboo sticks, and after shifting the heavy burden to the other shoulder away they would go again. Though their naked bodies would fairly shine with the sweat that trickled down their backs, yet they went great distances without apparent fatigue, always shouting to each other in keeping step. There were half-way stations on the mountain where they would stop to rest and eat rice; it is very amusing to see a dozen of their nude bodies dancing around the fire, each carrying a steaming bowl of rice in one hand and chop-sticks in the other.

Their appetites are well earned, and after eating plenty, they finish off with a cup of tea.

In coming down hill the coolies trot very fast, and jolt one almost to pieces; but on level ground the kango goes easily, and when you get accustomed to keeping your legs tied up in knots for two or three hours at a time, and are reconciled to wearing an artificial stiff neck for the same period, it becomes quite comfortable, and you can soon imagine yourself being rocked to sleep.

On the pass, we encountered naked runners, or post-carriers, with their broad-brimmed hats and their little post-boxes slung on a stick over their shoulders. There are the swift-footed fellows who afterwards brought me my home mails from Yokohama.

After ascending several thousand feet, through thickly wooded ravines, we reached the picturesque village of Hakone, nestled among the mountains, at the head of a lovely lake of the same name. The whole vicinity of Lake Hakone is perfectly charming, and I used to frequently stop here afterwards, as it was the "halfway" point between Shidz-u-o-ka and Yokohama.

The lake is six miles long, and the water is blue, clear, and cool; at one end of the lake is a small peninsula, and near it are the thatched roofs of the Hakone village, close by the shore. They look like white patches in the distance. A clump of trees behind the peninsula marks the spot where the road comes down the hill-slope, through a grand avenue of pines and poplars, and enter the village near an ancient guardhouse that used to be the military "key" of northern and eastern Japan. Only the foundations of this guardhouse now remain. The whole village of Hakone, like many of the town scattered along the "Tokaido," is located entirely on one street. The houses are plain wooden huts with paper sliding doors, matted floors on which people eat and sleep, and roofs covered with thatched straw, without chimneys, and having holes at the top to let out the smoke. Babies were sprawling around on the floors, or strapped upon their mother mothers' backs like an Indian papoose. Sometimes the baby's head was shaved, with tufts of hair left upon the sides and back of the head; at other times the child wore a little red cap, which I used to think quite pretty until I found it signified small-pox!

The "hotel" at Hakone was like most of the others we stopped at on the Tokaido; the landlord was very polite, and the women of the house favored us with loud demonstrations of welcome by uttering a chorus of strange sounds we could not understand.

Our coolies turned us out of the kangos on the porch of the hotel as though we had been in wheelbarrows; and taking off our shoes, as all Japanese do on entering the house, we walked across the clean straw mats to the inner apartment prepared for us.

Japanese houses are only one or two stories high, but cover a great deal of space, and have many rooms, separated from each other by framework and sliding doors covered simply with rice paper. All these sliding doors can be thrown open at once, making one large hall, so that from the street you can look straight through the house to the garden behind. The kitchen is at the very entrance, so that in coming in you pass through an array of pots and kettles, and see women boiling rice and frying fish over a fire kindled on the floor, or in a stone fireplace where there is no chimney. Unsavory odors greet you of unmentionable Japanese dishes, and you are glad to escape the smell by retiring to your room, which faces upon a small garden; here you sit upon the floor and rest as well as you can, in the absence of beds, chairs, sofas, or common comforts. My cook prepared supper from the preserved provisions brought with us in tin cans, and everything was served on tiny little tables, scarcely a foot high, in dishes no larger than saucers.

After tea, soft quilts were spread upon the floor of the guest chamber, which is one foot higher than the other rooms, and a wooden pillow-block with a little round roll on top of it was placed at the head of my pile of quilts for a pillow! When I placed my neck on the pillow-block I felt as if I were about to be decapitated; but they covered me with a great stuffed quilt, shaped like a coat, with arms two feet wide that flapped over me.

Then they hoisted a great mosquito net, and tucked the edges under me to keep away the rats! I wondered at this, until I rolled from under the net, and found the rats at midnight playing tag over my face! Nor could I drive the creatures away until I struck a match, when they fled at the light.

At one of the villages we afterwards passed, the yaconims mourned greatly that in the whole place they could not find silk comforters for me to sleep in, so that for one night I had to condescend to cotton ones. Everywhere we met with the most marked attention and respect; couriers went ahead to "prepare the way," and officials vied with each other in courtesy to the stranger.

We left Hakone Lake early the next morning, descending a portion of the way on foot. It is customary to start off while yet dark, so as to get well on the journey before the heat of the day. We had the path illuminated by huge torches made of bundles of dried reeds, which burned with a brilliant light, and were carried in advance by the coolies. It was a very weird sight: we wended our way through the dark forest and deep ravines, lighting up the rocks and trees, and causing shadows to flit along our path as the torches flared up or smoldered away in the hands of our guides. Ere long the morning light came creeping quietly over the neighboring hills, chasing away the gray mist and shooting long bright streaks across the sky, until at last the golden fringe of the eastern sun, which skirted the mountaintop, gave place to one broad dazzling flash of light, and the king of the day was ushered in with a perfect sea of glory. There was real romance in this early morning ramble, so far away from the rest of the world, with such strange and beautiful surroundings. We were now passing close along the foot of Fujiyama, and could see all the way up his sloping and regular sides, even to the spotless nightcap, which he still kept on his crater-like head. The first thing that would strike a Yankee boy on being brought up close to Fujiyama would be the jolly sliding place it would make from top to bottom for his winter sled; in fact, it looks as if it were shaved off for some such purpose, as well as to fit nicely on lacquer boxes and tea chests. The appearance of the Tokaido throughout this section of the country is splendid; it is lined all the way by a double row of massive and magnificent pines, whose overhanging branches have shaded the generations that have journeyed over this road for centuries. These old trees are among the most pleasing and interesting features of the whole country, and I like to hear the wind sighing through them, as though it were mourning over some strange and unknown scenes of the past. Passing through the villages so early, it was a peculiar sight to see all the houses shut up in front, their weather-beaten sliding doors fitting into each other so closely as to make the whole town look like a succession of windowless barns. Now and then, we met some old woman taking her morning walk, who was petrified with astonishment at the sudden apparition that greeted her.

Smoke issued from numberless crevices in the roofs, showing that the morning fires were being lighted within.

We stopped at a large teahouse, where breakfast was served in better style than usual, and then we reclined on the broad veranda overlooking a garden where dwarfed trees, miniature mountains, and rippling cascades were all placed in an incredibly small compass. We fed the finny tribe in the goldfish pond close to the veranda, and then sent out for "Jin-reka-shas," or man-power carriages, and resumed our journey southward. The "Jin-reka-sha" is a two-wheeled vehicle, more than twice the size of a substantial baby carriage, and is usually drawn by two men. One man gets into the thills, the other runs ahead with a rope. Both are finely tattooed with pictures pricked into the skin with ink of various colors. These pictures are similar to those seen on traditional Japanese fans, but are more elegantly executed. The naked bodies of these human horses are browned by the sun, and you study the muscular proportions of their powerfully developed limbs as they dash along the level road at a rate that fairly takes your breath away. By changing your men frequently you may have new pictures on their backs continually dancing before your eyes; and the varieties in art may thereby keep pace with the ever-changing beauties of nature through which you are passing! These fellows are very strong and I have often had a single pair of them carry me forty miles on a stretch!

They would stop every three hours to eat rice and refresh themselves; in this way, they would run a whole day without showing signs of weariness.

The little carriage has a cushioned seat and short springs, but in going down hill where the road is worn rough from the rains, you are liable to be bounced out if not very careful. Should a storm come up, you are protected from the wet, by an oiled silk top drawn up over your head, completely covering you; through a little flap you can look out at the storm and see your coolies with dripping straw coats splashing through the mud.

We were now approaching the seashore skirting the head of the deep Gulf of Su-run-ga, which bears the same name as the province where I was destined to live. On our right towered the great snowy peak of Fujiyama, nearly twelve thousand feet in height. All about us were waving fields of grain, white for the harvest; bright landscapes met the eye in every direction; fleecy clouds decked the mountainside; and sunlight and beauty filled the soul with joy, until some sad evidences of heathenism were passed, showing that though in the midst of God's bounties, we were still in pagan country.

The long journey drew to a close as we approached the suburbs of Shidz-u-o-ka. Several turbulent rivers had been crossed in flatboats, propelled by bamboo poles, and now the last relay of Jinrekashas had been given up, and we found ourselves entering the city, mounted upon jet-black Japanese ponies sent to us by the local officials. The directors of the Scientific School met us some distance down the road, and bade us welcome.

The streets of the city were crowded with people anxious to catch the first glimpse of the strange-looking foreigner. All traffic was cleared to the side streets, and the crowds were hushed into silence, as we rode slowly and in state toward the "ken-cho," or government house, where the official reception was to be given. Multitudes of faces peered at us from behind the sliding doors, and from rows of people squat on their heels by the wayside as we marched by. Crossing the drawbridge of the castle moat, we passed under an immense gate, and then turned toward an enclosure filled with spacious buildings.

We dismounted at the second gate, and walked across a paved court-yard to a broad porch where twenty or thirty officials stood waiting to receive us. I could immediately see by the demeanor of my guards and attendants, and by their profound bows, that I was in some very august presence; for they had received quite complacently all the salutations on the journey, but now they bobbed and scraped as though they could not get their heads low enough!

The "Gon-dai-san-je," governors of the province of Su-run-ga, welcomed me with all the dignity due their station, and after taking off my hat and boots, I walked up to them and bowed respectfully. They returned the salutation, and the, without a word being spoken, conducted me into an inner chamber, where a brand new table with two plain wooden chairs had been provided. The chief official sat down with me, while all the rest stood by, and our first "interview" proceeded through interpreters; the French language being used, which was then translated into Japanese.

The governors welcomed me, they said, to the province and city over which they ruled, and congratulated me upon the auspicious termination of the long and tiresome journey from my distant home. They expressed themselves particularly pleased that I had arrived in Japan so much sooner than they expected.

I replied that in America, we were accustomed to do things very promptly, and that no sooner was their invitation received than I acted upon it. They seemed grateful and satisfied.

After further conversation, they said I must be weary after my long ride, so they ordered my attendants to escort me to the great temple, which was hereafter to be my "home"!

Chapter 3

Life In A Buddhist Temple

The Buddhist temples usually occupy the most picturesque sites, enshrined among thickly shaded groves, and secluded from the noise and bustle of the large cities. Approaching them through an avenue of trees, or ascending the hill slope, you may see their massive roofs, carved pagodas, and huge bell towers rising abruptly through the green foliage. The very atmosphere of sacred solitude surrounds them.

In one of these temples, I was destined to live during my first year in Japan. With all its heathen rites and pagan darkness, I yet learned to call it my home. Under almost the same roof with me were the priests of Buddha and the idols, before whom incense was continually burning, filling the house with fragrance. The grounds of the temple covered several acres, and contained nearly a dozen buildings. Some of the shrines, and the central building was a temple and dwelling combined. Here most of the worship was performed by day and night, and here I lived.

Several massive gates led into the grounds. Under the largest stood two grim warriors, carved in wood and painted plaster, measuring fifteen feet in height, and holding giant spears, bows, and arrows, with which to guard the sacred portals of the temple. Colossal pines shaded the walks, and bamboo groves skirted the hillside. To the left stood a Buddhist cemetery on the terraced slope of the hill. A great bronze bell in the tower tolled solemnly and slow, with a deep booming sound, every evening when the sun went down.

At first I thought it quite romantic; I liked the retirement and the peaceful stillness, broken only by the prayers of the priests and the measured beat of the drums accompanying the repetition of the musical words, "Buddha amida" and "Na-mi-o-ho-ren-gi-ko."[27] The priests were very polite, and sent me fresh tea raised in their own garden, and boxes of eggs and sponge-cake. I thanked them, sent them some preserved peaches, and invited them to attend my Bible class!

In fact, I *had* a Bible-class, even in this stronghold of heathenism, with nothing to interrupt except the noises of the gongs and the pagan worship of the adjoining temple. On the very Sabbath, at the request of many of my brightest pupils, I explained the teachings of Christianity to as earnest and intelligent a young men as it was ever my privilege to address. They listened for more than two hours to a careful presentation of Christian truth, warmly thanking me at the close, and gladly accepted a copy of the Scriptures, which I gave each one of them, promising to study the chapter assigned for the next Sabbath.

The happiest memories I have connected with my long exile in the interior of Japan are those of the hours regularly spent with my Sabbath-morning

---

[27] Nam-myoho-renge-kyo, the chant of Buddhists of the Nichiren school.

Bible-class. The eagerness with which the truth was received, the affectionate gratitude mani-fested by all who attended, the solemn assurance which the Divine Spirit gave of his presence, and the consciousness that I was present-ing Christ to those who had never known him, but would soon rejoice in his salvation, filled me with awe and yet with enthusiasm, and gave; an unction to my words far above the secular teachings of the weekday lecture-room or laboratory. Of the difficulties experienced in presenting spiritual truth to minds entirely unaccustomed to it, and through a strange language, I need not speak; but all obstacles were gradually overcome, and the students would write me grateful notes during the week, asking questions on the subject dis-cussed, and usually closing with short exclamations like the following:

"These are golden truths you are giving us, and they satisfy the soul," said one student. " I have got very great important points yesterday, of which you have spoken to us from the faith, " wrote another. A third wrote, " Alas! My grandmother has died without knowing the greatness and glory of our God, and the comfort of the blessed Gospel of our Savior Jesus Christ."

So engrossing were my duties during the week that it was impossible for me to meet the students more than once for systematic Bible study. But they became so interested in the subject that they voluntarily started a Japanese Bible-class, conducted by themselves; the class was held on every Sunday afternoon, at the house of one of their number, and the Chinese and Japanese translations of the Scriptures were used.

Shi-mo-jo, my favorite interpreter, lived with me at the temple; he was the brightest and most interesting young Japanese I ever met, and I learned to love him as a brother. He was invaluable to me in a thousand ways, and I bestowed great care on his education. In scientific studies, he made rapid progress, and at my daily lectures in the classroom, he rendered the work of instruction delightful by the clearness and enthusiasm with which he would expound to others the most abstruse scientific subjects.

But his health was delicate, and to my great sorrow he died in his twenty-fourth year, just as he was entering a life full of usefulness and promise. Over his grave, in a Japanese cemetery in Tokyo, was raised a large stone, with a touching inscription written in Chinese by his friend Nakamura ; and having at the close a complete statement of the Christian faith, in the hope and comfort of which Shimojo died.

Two little boys also lived with me; one was the son of Governor Okubo, and the other the sort of the captain of a Japanese ship-of-war, which went down in the last naval battle fought in 1868 by the forces of the Tycoon. When the father of this little boy saw that his ship was going to sink, he sent his men away in the boats, and then set the ship on fire, and drew his sword and committed "h'a-ra-ki-ru," which the Japanese consider a very brave and honorable way of terminating life.

I must not forget to mention another humble member of my house-hold, who had quite a remarkable history even before I became acquainted with him. His name was " Sam Patch "! and he was my cook. He was nearly twice as old as any of the rest of us, and used to amuse us with his droll style and strange stories.

"Sam" was formerly a poor Jap sailor-boy, who drifted to sea in a terrible periodical storm - the "typhoon," which drove his frail junk far away from the shore. After many anxious days on the ocean he was picked up by an American sailing vessel and carried to San Francisco. Here he was friendless and alone, so he embarked on another ship and went to China, and after-wards to the Philippine Islands. When Commodore Perry went to Japan to make the first treaty, he took Sam on his flag-ship, the Mississippi; but as Sammy was afraid of losing his head if he landed, he fell on his face before Commodore Perry, and begged him to bring him back to America. In those days the Japanese were so barbarous in their feelings toward foreign-ers that they would even kill any of their own people who had been among foreigners and then come back again. Sammy was therefore permitted to take the long voyage around Cape Horn to New York, and it was on this journey that the sailors nicknamed him " Sam Patch," as they could not pronounce his real, Japanese name, San-ta-ro.

Sammy was befriended by a missionary, who took him to his home in the central part of New York State. On their way Sam passed through Albany and Syracuse, which he afterwards described to me as very queer places. Sam had great opportunities in the world, but he didn't have any brains to start on; so after a while he was sent back to Japan, where he aspired to the position of "cook," in various missionary families. He liked to have his own way, however, and after many vicissitudes, he became the chief of my kitchen department. He baked the bread, roasted the ducks, made pies and puddings, and his ricecakes were everywhere famous. Finally, at the end of three years, I buried him in a Buddhist cemetery; but of that, I will speak by and by.

Perhaps you may wonder how I occupied myself during these long months away from society and civilization, without seeing an American or European face for half a year at a time.

You may even imagine that I had an easy and dreamy existence, in the midst of shady trees, fragrant incense, and oriental repose. On the contrary, I never before worked half so hard as I did during the months of exile in the interior of Japan. With an institution of nearly one thousand students, under the supervision of a single foreigner; with fifty Japanese assistants to direct and instruct; with classes in various scientific departments, both theoretical and practical; with interpreters to be drilled, regulations to be made and enforced, experiments prepared, and lectures given through the threefold medium of English, French, and Japanese, you may believe I had my hands full.

My regular duties at the school began on Christmas day, as much time had been spent in getting settled. During Christmas week the heathen festival occurred of offering first-fruits of the earth to the pagan deities, so that three holidays were given. We began again on New Year's Day, and I made out a program of studies, which was accepted and printed in Japanese. I said nothing respecting the Sabbath, but left the space blank; the officials inferred my wishes, however, and inserted the word "rest." It was quietly done, and an order was issued changing the previous arrangements, and closing the school on the Sabbath.

I usually rose at six o'clock in the morning, and after breakfast the horses and guards would appear at the gate. Passing across the little garden, with its dwarfed trees and goldfish pond, I would mount my jet black Japanese pony and gallop down the road, preceded by my "bet-to," or groom, and followed by the guard. The " bet- to" was a well-formed young fellow, naked to the waist, and splendidly tattooed with colored figures and dragons; he ran like a deer, and always kept ahead of the horse, clearing the road by a peculiar cry, which made everybody get out of the way. The distance from my temple to the school building was more than a mile, and as I frequently went over the ground four times a day, it was sometimes necessary to go very fast.

When I got tired of riding horseback - for the Jap ponies are very spirited and hard to hold - I borrowed a four-wheeled foreign carriage, which I found the ex-Tycoon[28] had brought to the city. This carriage was the only one in the whole province, and was a great curiosity to the Japanese. It had been presented by the Dutch, to the Tycoon, and now that it was no longer needed, he lent it to me, with the horse that had been trained to the harness. But Shidz-u-o-ka roads were never made for carriages, so the governors caused the way to be widened by building new bridges and small embankments.

If you could have seen the bewildered amazement of the natives as my chariot wheels dashed by their doors, you would suppose something frightful was coming. Mothers were running for their babies in the middle of the road, peasants flying into the ditches, ducks cackling, dogs barking, and stones rattling-all mingling in the wild *melee*. Yet nobody was hurt.

The two-sworded men[29] on the road would prostrate themselves before the carriage, thinking that the ex-Tycoon was coming; but when they heard the laughter of my guards as we passed, they looked very fierce and

---

[28] "Tycoon" was the word used for the former Tokugawa Shoguns who were exiled to their native Shizuoka when the Shogunate was overthrown by the new Meiji government in 1868.

[29] samurai

straightened up immediately. They were as wrathful in the end as they were reverential in the beginning. These were the men who disliked foreigners.

To reach the school building we had to pass a drawbridge crossing a deep moat, which skirted the outer embankment of the old castle grounds. Then riding a quarter of a mile through the enclosure, we passed under a wooden gate, and dismounted at the school. Here the directors and petty officials would meet us.

At the side entrance of the school are shelves upon which are ranged hundreds of wooden clog-shoes, which the scholars have taken off on entering; instead of a hat-rack (of which there would be no need), you see a sword-rack, with pegs in it, upon which rows of small swords are resting, some of which are sharp and elegantly ornamented. These belong to the Samurai scholars within, who, though small, are proud of their rank, and are entitled to wear swords in their little belts, with the ancient family crest on their clothing.

On entering the part of the building where Japanese instruction is going on in the old-fashioned style, you hear a great buzzing sound, such as might come from a colossal beehive, and as the noise gets louder and louder you can distinguish the shrill voices of several hundred youngsters, who seem to vie with one another in studying aloud their Chinese and Japanese lessons.

Following the dignified steps of the director, you pass through various rooms with low ceilings and matted floors, finding in each room rows of tables a foot high, before which squat the little folks upon straw mats. The noise subsides somewhat as you enter the room, and all the scholars bow down in an instant before you, touching either the table or the floor with their foreheads. Each teacher greets you with" 0-hi-o! " (Good morning) and kneels beside you while inspecting the class, catching every glance of commendation you deign to give, and as you retire he draws a deep sigh, not of relief but of respect, and the next class goes through the same formality.

In the school and the family the children are trained to politeness and respect to their superiors as the first and most essential requirement; and the dignified and gentle manner in which the young folks conduct themselves is really surprising. The Japanese are the most polite people in the world, and though they have bare feet and wear less clothing than we do in America, they certainly are more courteous and kind than many people who call themselves " civilized." The children especially are never quarrelsome or troublesome ; they are obedient and dutiful to parents and teachers, and are all the happier for it. In the school, you would not see any thing that even approached disorder, and there was an air of refinement about the commonest-clad child. The scholars wore loose dresses with long sleeves, which served as pockets, and in which they carried tops, strings, oranges, and rolls of brown paper, or any thing they needed. They tied up their books in pieces of cotton or silk, and carried them home to study at night in the same noisy way. All this loud study of former days simply filled their heads with long passages from classical Chinese and Japanese books, which they memorized by rote, without understanding half they studied. They had to learn a great many " moral precepts" also, such as obedience to parents and the elder brother, respect for the aged, worship at the graves of their ancestors, offerings at the shrines of pagan gods, and stories of romance and robbers, which were calculated to teach bravery and give them contempt of death.

The scholars in the Japanese and Chinese department came to school at six o'clock in the morning and were dismissed at nine. They also came again at five in the afternoon. My own classes of the more advanced students commenced at nine o'clock and continued until noon; then I arranged the apparatus and experiments in the new laboratory built for me, preparatory to the afternoon lectures, which began at two o'clock and continued until five.

I wrote chemical formulas, and drew diagrams on the large blackboard, which were copied by the students while I went home to dinner. On returning, I would find fifty or sixty young men seated in the large lecture-room, ready for the experiments and the lecture in chemistry or physics. These young men were nearly all about my own age, enthusiastic in their pursuit of science, and diligent in their studies to a degree that astonished me. They mastered with facility textbooks that had taxed all the energies of American college students, and were so thorough and devoted to their work that it was a pleasure to teach them.

The government had been very liberal in providing suitable scientific and philosophical apparatus, so that all the principles and problems in chemistry and physics could be proved and illustrated before their eyes. The experiments were at times a little dangerous, but the Japanese delight in excitement, and would face without fear the most hazardous "demonstrations."

One may easily imagine with what astonishment and delight these people (who had hitherto known nothing of science and the marvelous inventions of our age) viewed for the first time the wonders of electricity, the steam-engine, the air-pump, the startling results of chemical combinations, and all the powers and appliances of modern physics. No wonder that rumors floated about among the common people outside the school that either I had "the gods" or "the devil" in my laboratory, they didn't know which! While I was performing my experiments, Shimojo, my interpreter, would explain the principles to those students who only understood Japanese; other students were taught in French or English. Between the three languages, we usually got along very well: they always asked a great many questions.

When the duties of the day were over, the horses and bettos would appear at the door, and I would ride home to tea. I always found " Sam Patch" awaiting me at the temple with hot rice-cakes and honey, and plenty of nice things. The guards put up at the little house at the gate, and as night came on the servants closed the long line of sliding-doors, which ran in grooves on three sides of the building, so that the whole temple was shut up like a box! No one could enter the grounds after dark.

At night I could hear the rats racing through the great empty lofts of the temple; hundreds of them would come scampering over the thin wooden ceiling at midnight, directly over my head, and I would wake up with a start, thinking that a small army was coming! Earthquakes are very frequent in Japan, and often occur at night. Sometimes I would be aroused from my sleep by a strange motion of the bed, as though its four legs were about to walk off with me! On listening, I would hear the heavy timbers in the roof creaking, and the whole building groaning and shivering like a ship at sea. Still, as there was no storm raging outside, I could not sometimes imagine what the commotion meant, until, on lying perfectly quiet, I could feel the earthquake waves passing under the temple at intervals of two or three minutes each. Usually there are three waves, and the second is the most severe; so, if the first shock was heavy enough to shake things up badly, I would scamper out of bed, and try and get from under the massive roof of the temple before the second wave would have a chance to bring it down on my head. These roofs, being made of stone tiles, are exceedingly heavy, and are supported simply by uprights standing on the ground, without any foundation; in fact, the whole building stands on wooden legs. As the earthquake wave passes under, these timbers slip and creak and make a great fuss, but do not fall. When they *do* fall, however, woe to the unfortunate people who happen to be underneath! In the destructive earthquake in Tokyo, some years ago, more than sixty thousand persons perished by the falling of these tiled roofs and the opening of deep crevices in the earth.

One Saturday, after I had returned from the school, the gatekeeper, knowing that some money had been left in the building, undertook to become robber instead of guard. He slipped quietly into the room where the money was, and finding one of the guards sleeping with his head resting on a pillow-block, he attempted to decapitate him. The poor fellow seized the sword blade in trying to save himself; but these Japanese weapons are as sharp as razors, and he only cut his fingers off. In another instant the robber had killed him and fled with the money, leaving a Buddhist book behind, which fell from his clothing. By this book he was afterwards detected in the next province, and brought back to Shidz-u-o-ka and beheaded. If it were not too terrible, I could describe the way they sometimes "try" such criminals by torture.

Earthquakes, robbers, and the romantic experiences of a strange country kept life in the old Buddhist temple free from monotony for some time; but at last it became very lonely, as the romance and novelty faded out, and the clatter of drums and gongs in the temple, instead of being musical, became intolerable. I used to wander up through the woods, passing the Buddhist burying-ground, and sit down on top of the hill (on every Sabbath afternoon), and took off across the Pacific towards home.

The sullen roar of the ocean could be heard as the waves broke heavily upon the beach five miles away; that same sea washed the shores of my own country, nearly five thousand miles further east. The sun set over the western hills of Japan, and reappeared rising from the ocean, fresh from its journey across the continent of America. It came to me bright and cheery every morning from "home," though all my distant friends were in bed and asleep in America at the time it reached me in Japan.

Still the days and months rolled by, and though I worked hard and kept busy, there were hours when the sense of loneliness seemed too oppressive to be borne. On the Sabbath especially I would pace to and fro on my temple porch, or climb alone to the hilltop, and think of the long months yet to come before I could hope to see a familiar face or hear a familiar American voice.

If I could only see a single foreigner like myself for "just a few minutes," I would often say, then I thought I would be happy and willing to stand another siege of seclusion from society. But when this did happen eventually, and two friends came all the way from Yokohama to visit me a few days, I felt all the more lonely after they left; for the solitude seemed more complete, in contrast to the merry social times which they said everybody was having in Yokohama and said everybody was having in Yokohama and Tokyo. Nevertheless I believe in solitude, and I like it, provided it comes in doses that can be endured. I believe that true development comes through some forms of solitude faster than through most forms of society.

One can be happy alone, if he has the proper resources within himself; and I looked back upon that old Buddhist temple as the brightest and happiest spot that I have yet seen in the world.

Chapter 4

Life in a Feudal Castle

Nearly three hundred years ago the founder of the Tycoon dynasty dwelt in a great castle. This castle was at Shidzuoka, and was surrounded with high walls and broad moats with water flowing through them. There was a double line of moats, stretching in a continuous circuit of half a mile or more, and faced with sold stone masonry. Within the inner enclosure, there rose a massive tower and other lesser battlements. Upon the long line of embankments, pine trees were planted, from which the archers might shoot their arrows at the foe. The trees were young then, but now are grand and stately in their old age. From these castle grounds, a most impressive view was presented on either hand. To the north stood the "Matchless Mountain," ever fresh and glorious in its snowy robes, and capped with more silvery clouds than ever shadowed an Alpine peak. On the west stood a long range of bleak heights, which opened up into a valley rich in fertility and every tint of green.

All around the castle was spread out a broad expanse of rice fields and waving grain, while a few miles to the east lay the ocean, whose distant roar could easily be heard, and whose waves had so long broken upon the shores of a land locked in mystery. The thatched-roof houses and huts of Shidzuoka (then called *Fitsiu,* or Chief Capital,) were scattered in great numbers about the castle; and all the inhabitants rendered complete submission and homage to their feudal lord, the First Tycoon. This castle is now in ruins, and fire and earthquake have left little there save the walls and moats and crumbled towers shaded by patriarchal pines. The mail-clad warriors are gone who once walked these now deserted parapets; the archers no longer shoot their arrows from the fir branches of the trees; the spearmen and swordsman who guarded the gates have gone to their graves long ago, leaving the copper-covered gates unbarred, the drawbridges tottering and decayed, and the wild foxes to roam among the ruins and vine-covered rocks of the once mighty fortress. For a century or more, these castle-grounds remained unoccupied, and the birds and wild animals had learned to make it their home; while the city still thrived without the walls, and grew in crescent form around the broad outer moat of the castle.

After I had lived a year at the Buddhist temple described in the last chapter, the government decided to build me a house in foreign style, and I was requested to select the most suitable site for its location. My two friends Katz and Okubo, who had been councilors in the court of the last Tycoon (and who were more recently instrumental in calling me to Japan), were the persons who built me the house, as a gift from San-mie-san, a little prince of the province, whom they had in charge. This little prince was greatly respected in the region, as he was descended from those who had ruled the country for three hundred years, and would have been the present Tycoon had not that power been overthrown.

Katz and Okubo thought my temple home too far away from the school and too unprotected, besides being inconvenient in many ways. They wisely proposed the new house, and I chose the deserted castle grounds as the best place upon which to build. The Japanese carpenters had never seen a foreign house, nor were they familiar with modern methods of construction; neither did I consider myself an architect, or capable of very explicit directions. But I wanted a house well built, comfortable, and secure. So we determined to overcome all obstacles. I drew up the plans with care, and for nearly six months hundreds of stonecutters and carpenters were engaged in executing them. A portion of the embankment on the corner of the castle moat was cut away and faced with solid masonry, constructed from stones drawn from the ruins of the old castle tower. The stones for the walls of the house were brought from a neighboring province.

I experienced much pleasure in watching the progress of my crude architectural ideas, as they slowly assumed solid reality. But the work was no child's play; for not only did the ground plan and apartments have to be mapped out, but every thing inside and outside the house had to be explained, for the Japs had no more idea of their meaning than the man in the moon. Doors, windows, stairs, closets, chimneys, and other minor details had to be drawn and presented to the head-carpenter by pictures and measurements. Sometimes the most amusing mistakes would occur, owing to his never having seen the objects in question. The carpenters were skillful in imitation beyond any thing you could believe. They brought back the most perfect little models of the things described, and it was seldom necessary to correct them.

After the work of building was fairly commenced, the *roof* was completed in a month, and the heaviest part of the foundation in two months more; for you must know that it would be decidedly contrary to Japanese character to do any thing except in a manner directly opposite to all our preconceived notions on the subject. In a Japanese house, the roof is always built first, and the other parts afterwards! With a kind of celestial instinct, they always commence at the highest point and work downwards. In all the lesser occupations of daily labor, such as digging, sawing, planing, cutting lumber, boring holes, or turning screws, the Japanese do just exactly the reverse of what people do on the other hemisphere; and it is consistent with the idea which children have at home respecting our antipodes, the queer folks that walk with their heads down and their feet sticking up, like flies on a ceiling.

After watching the manner in which they built the house, I felt as if they would be inclined to stand the whole thing on its chimneys, with kitchen and cellar skyward; but this was hardly convenient to do. The chimneys, by the way, were the most mysterious part of the house to the carpenters. For a long time they could not be prevailed upon to build them; but at last they broke holes through the floors and roof, and, with the aid of the stone-cutters, put them in. They regarded the building of the house as a wonderful achievement, and hundreds of people from all over the country came to see it, supposing that all houses in America were built in the same style.

The picture given of the house is taken from inside the castle grounds. On the right of the picture is a small Japanese house occupied by "Sam Patch," who is seen standing in front. The well is also seen with the stone furnace where Sam heated the water for baths. In the foreground is Japanese well, with a long bamboo stick, having stone tied at the end, like the old Egyptian method of drawing water.

Four large pine trees stand near the house, between which I used to suspend a beautiful American flag, which the Japanese called the " flower flag," and which could be seen from the surrounding country. With it waved a small Japanese flag, having the "rising sun" upon it; the American " stars" and the Japanese "sun" floated very peacefully together, and in raising the flags I usually caused salutes to be fired. The situation of the house was very picturesque. It stood upon the outer embankment of the castle moat, facing northward upon the " Matchless Mountain" of Japan; to the left, towards the sun setting, were fertile valleys and verdant hills; and to the south - the side on which the picture is taken-its open outlook was towards the ruins and interior moats of the castle. On the south side of the house a court-yard is seen, where I gave a " stereopticon exhibition"[30] on Christmas eve to several hundred delighted Japanese, the parents and friends of my students. The evening was beautiful, and the people came early with printed tickets that invited them to " a trip in imagination through foreign countries and the starry heavens"!

Not the least interesting part of the entertainment to them was the opportunity given of viewing the interior of my house. Ushers were appointed to guide them around, and for an hour the people poured in and out of the house, uttering all manner of exclamations of wonder at what they saw. And well they might, for the poor creatures had never been accustomed in their own homes to any thing we would call comfort. Living and sleeping, as they do, on straw mats, in simple wooden houses with paper windows and shutters, and without any thing that we could call furniture, except little lacquer tables a foot high, of course a foreign house, furnished in American style, appeared to them luxurious beyond description.

They examined every object with the minutest care; carpets, rocking chairs, table-covers, writing desk, mirrors, face curtains, chandelier, beds, and bureaus-all were of great novelty to them. The brilliant colored oil-cloth in the hall created astonishment as they walked upon it, for they could not imagine what it was or how it could be made. The walls and ceilings were covered with bright-tinted paper of various patterns - for we do not use plaster ceilings in this land of earthquakes and the Japanese understood the wall paper very well, for it is from Japan that Europeans first got the idea of covering their walls with paper.

But when the Japs, especially the ladies, came to explore the kitchen, their admiration for the cooking-range and chimney was unbounded.

---

[30] akin to the modern slide show.

They had never seen ovens, or appliances for baking, roasting, etc., and everything in the culinary department was a revelation to them exceeding the novelties of the parlor, bedrooms, or well-stocked pantry.

When it was dark I seated the people on straw mats in the courtyard, and delighted them with the stereopticon entertainment. They had never seen such a sight before, and the beautiful pictures of scenes in America and Europe were like glimpses into another world. The revolving astronomical diagrams excited great astonishment. I tried to prove by the shadow of the earth on the moon, and by the ship sailing around the globe, that our world was round. But the old folks shook their heads, and were skeptical on that point; for they had been in the world longer than I had, and *knew* it was flat!

After most of the people had gone home, I gave a Christmas dinner - or supper rather - to forty of my friends and the officers of the province. The long tables, bountifully spread, proved a climax upon their astonishment and their appetites, and they pronounced the bill of fare as good as it was novel. There were roast ducks and chickens, corn, peas, beans, tomatoes, succotash, and potatoes, besides plenty of pies, cakes, jellies, and sweetmeats. All of these foreign provisions were imported from London and San Francisco. The Japanese market is limited to rice, fish, and a few unpalatable vegetables. Piles of oranges, apples, and other fruit loomed up among the casters and dishes, and the long white tables, lit up by lamps and countless candies, presented a cheery appearance, rendered doubly gay by the reflection of the large mirror hanging on the wall.

After half an hour the provisions began to grow beautifully less, and the clatter of unskillful knives and forks became less apparent. At this stage of the proceedings a large turkey appeared upon the scene, and was of course the rarest sight of all. Said turkey had been presented to me some time previous by one of the Daisanje, and had been purchased by him at a fabulous price from some enterprising Japanese, who had brought it from Yokohama, but had found it "a white elephant" upon his hands. I had kept and fattened my feathered friend especially for this Christmas occasion;

and when he came in well stuffed and plump, with oyster-sauce accompaniment, I indulged the hope that I might strategically remove a nice slice or a "drumstick" to my own plate for private purposes. I had, moreover, ordained that two or three "courses" should intervene before the bringing on of the turkey, trusting thereby to stay the tide of demolition, so that when it came to turkey it would have to say, "Thus far, and no farther." But alas! vain was the hope for me and my drumsticks! The sight of the turkey only renewed their courage, and they set to work again with greater vigor. I was kept so busy carving that I had no time to realize that friend turkey was fast disappearing from my view, until when I at last came to my senses not a vestige remained save a few stuffing crumbs and that unmentionable appendage which goes over the fence last.

The only amusement I had as the long months passed away was in entertaining the Japanese and seeing them enjoy themselves. On various holidays, I would give them dinners, scientific experiments, fireworks, or exhibitions with the microscope and the stereopticon. In return they would deluge me with presents and with expressions of gratitude, and take me to see any Japanese display that they supposed worth showing.

One of the students came to me one day and said there was a great Japanese "tournament " going on on the other side of the castle, and that it was like the " War of the Roses" which he had read of in English history, and like one which Japanese feudal history also tells about. So I went off with him, thinking it was a good chance to see the style of warfare, which once prevailed, about the very castle in which I was then living. We found a spacious enclosure, fitted up like a; great circus ring, with a frail bamboo balcony running around it, upon which the spectators were seated. The first part of the fray consisted of single combats, in which the knights were arrayed in old-fashioned armor, the same as that worn in past feudal days. Instead of steel swords, however, they used a clumsy bamboo weapon shaped like a sword; for they did not intend killing each other, though they struck very heavy blows. Before each pair of combatants engaged each other, a personage in flowing robes, and with a large black fan, would step forward and announce their names in a most ridiculous tone of voice, and then holding his open fan out towards them he bade them approach each other. Whereupon they advanced to the center of the ring and saluted, and then, wetting the handles of their swords with water, went to work.

First, they began fencing, until one attempted either a thrust or a blow, and then there came such a clatter and quick succession of foils and strokes that you could scarcely see who was getting the worst of it. Usually a fair and square blow on the head would settle the question, and one of the "braves" would jump backward with a triumphant yell. The person who got fairly struck twice out of three times was declared defeated, and a "judge" always stood by to decide any point in dispute.

The main feature of the show came about the middle of the afternoon, and it was this, which my interpreter had called a little " War of the Roses. "After a general clearing up of every thing for the coming strife, forty "knights" appeared upon the field, each with his armor, sword, and a hideous-looking mask. They were heralded by a trumpeter, who came with stately step into the middle of the ring, dressed in a rich white robe of silk, and carrying his horn in a silken net. This horn was a superb instrument, made from a natural seashell, and the notes it yielded were mournfully beautiful. My interpreter said this was the horn used in olden times to call the people to battle. So, as the notes of the horn died away, the forty knights began to file into the field for action.

First came the "Whites" all clad in armor, each having a white sash or ribbon tied over his head, and streaming down behind. In the center stood their color-bearer, not with a flag, as you would suppose, but with three great plume-shaped things dancing over his helmet. Next came the "Reds," their chief walking in front with stately tread, and their red ribbons shaking in anticipation of the bloody fray. They too had a color-bearer of the same tripod style, and when he shook his head the scarlet banner waved like a tree in the wind. But the two parties did not stand long on ceremony; the line of battle was formed, and though it was of limited extent it made the conflict all the closer. Each party kept a reserve in the rear, and each color-bearer was also kept be- hind. Each knight had upon the top of his helmet a small piece of soft wood, tied loosely with a string.

Inasmuch as it was inexpedient for them to break each other's *heads* in the fight, the next best thing they could do was to break this little piece of *wood* on top of the head. Whoever had his little piece of wood broken was considered as getting the equivalent of having his head smashed, and was therefore placed *hors du combat,* and must leave the ring!

The Japs are very polite, even in fighting, so the first thing the two lines of warriors did was to salute each other, and then, at a signal from their chiefs, they sprang upon each other like tigers. Such a *melee* as ensued I never before saw. There were shouts and yells, and rushing to and fro, and crashing of swords and sticks, and torn ribbons fluttering in the wind, till it became one bewildered scene of tumult and confusion.

For some time we could not tell which party would come out ahead, though one individual after another was seen leaving the ring with his hel- met off and his piece of wood broken. But at last the "Reds" rushed into the reserve of the "Whites," and it looked as though things were getting rather hot for the latter. Nevertheless the "Whites" rallied and drove the "Reds" into their own camp, and then the scene was most exciting.

The crash of arms had reached its height, and scarcely a thing was to be seen save the dozens of uplifted swords which rose and fell repeatedly, mak- ing one think the Japs must have pretty thick skulls to withstand such a continuous thumping. But at last the color-bearer of the "Reds" got his tri- pod standard broken, and nearly half his comrades had already been driven from the field. So the fray ceased, and the "Whites" gave a shout of victory!

The open area of the castle was very much exposed to storms, and the elevated position of my new house gave me the full benefit of thunder and lightning, and sometimes of a typhoon. One Friday night we had a most terrific thunderstorm. It awoke the whole city from sleep, and at midnight raged with such fury as to threaten the frail Japanese houses with destruc- tion. The rain poured in torrents, and was driven in every direction by the wind. The flashes of lightning followed each other with such rapidity and dazzling brightness that the whole neighborhood was one blaze of light, and the thunder shook the earth with its repeated reverberations. Such a succession of flashes I never saw-first here, then there, then everywhere, lighting up the sky with a ghastly and insupportable glow. The clouds were black and heavy, hanging very near the earth, while thunder and lightning came so close that sound and flash blended into each other with a rattle and roar that shook the house and bed on which I lay, causing me to quake in sympathy with them. The lightning struck a tall "fireproof " storehouse near by, setting it in a blaze notwithstanding the pouring rain. This building belonged to a covetous and rich old man, who kept all his goods locked up here, secure from fire or robbers from without; but the Japanese afterwards said that the fire of heaven "fell into" the storehouse for his withholding from the poor the food they so much needed.

I often thought of placing a lightning rod on one of the tall trees near my house, as the position was very much exposed; but the Jap carpenter had never heard of such a contrivance for "catching fire from heaven," and I could not prevail upon him to put one up. The storm finally passed off to the northeast, marking its course with the same vivid forks of light; white behind it left the blazing building, whose flames leaped higher and higher as the rain ceased, lighting up the scene with a different kind of glare.

The deep-toned gongs of the various temples chimed in one after the other, giving their musical but mournful signals of the fire alarm. At one time it looked as though the conflagration would become general, like another fire we had a short time before, which laid waste quite a section of the city. But the " fireproof " walls were thick and massive, and served to keep the flames enclosed, though they towered to a great height. As I looked about the outskirts of the castle walls, everybody was turning out to the fire, and for a time there was a perfect procession of men and lanterns passing the house. But, true to their Jap instinct, there was no haste or hurry. They were as slow about this as about everything else, and they all walked as though it would have been a sin for them to run even to a fire.

Soon the fire flickered away, darkness came again, and was only broken when the sun rose and gave us the morning as bright and clear as the night had been dark and terrible.

I close this chapter with a letter written by my good missionary friend, Rev. James Ballagh, of Yokohama, who came to see me in the summer of 1873, and who sent home an interesting description of the surroundings and historical associations of my house within the old Tycoon's castle.

" *HIDZUOKA, JAPAN, September 2, 1873.*

"Yes, here I am, after a week's journey through baffling storms and floods.

"We were storm-stayed two days at Fujiyam[31]a, spent a day and a night in a hut on the mountains, and were detained, day and a half by flooded rivers, yet we had a very enjoyable time. What with the company we fell in with, and the abundance and variety of good cheer provided in the shape of preserved meats and fruits, we have not lacked what was requisite to stay up the outer or inner man.

"I set out with brother Clark, partly to make experience of his trials in living in the interior, partly for a change, and partly to visit the homes and families of some of my Christian pupils, whose fathers reside at this place; and my highest anticipations have been more than realized.

"I feel grateful to my Heavenly Father for what his hand has here wrought. Let materialists try to legislate God out of his own universe, they cannot put him out of his wonder-working providence, nor out of the joyous confidence of the humblest believer. I feel this conviction very strongly here in this Christian home and its surroundings. It is located in the province of Surunga, which boasts not only of its' peerless' Fujiyama, but of being the birth-place and home of Ieasu, the founder of the last dynasty of Tycoons. He was not only a great general, the friend and ally of the Great Taiko Sarna - the George Washington of Japan - but was his successor in the government. This was his ancient capital. Here was his castle. Later he built Yedo, and made that the great northern

---

[31] Mt. Fuji.

capital of Japan. To it he brought together all the princes of the empire; there he compelled them to build palaces, and reside half of their time, alternating between the provinces and the capital. There he instituted a system of court etiquette, of counter-checks in government, etc. that truly entitled him to the appellation of the Jefferson of Japan. After his death he was buried at Kuno, near Shidzuoka, and here, at the splendid temples erected in his memory, he was worshipped as Great Go Ngen Sama.

"What makes his memory most important to us is that he formed the laws against Christianity that have existed without change for nearly three centuries. His predecessor, Taiko, persecuted the converts, and by the third Tycoon, they were exterminated.

"His last successor, the seventeenth from Ieasu, now lives here in exile.

"Now the evidence that this is of God is shown by the remarkable change of government that took place when the last Tycoon was in the height of his power, and the results that have followed strike the most incredulous as the wonderful work of God.

"Here is my friend's home - the house a perfect gem of beauty and durability in itself, occupied by a young, joyous, decided Christian, with every room in it emblazoned with mottoes - located within Ieasu's old castle grounds, as a tower of Christianity and civilization, on the very corner of the moat! And there, if you lack further proof of what God has wrought, raise your eye to that well-filled bookcase standing in the room in which I write, with one shelf entirely filled with Bibles, and the others with works of 'science and religion'; while above the bookcase stands one of the board tablets on which is written the old edict against Christianity, and which by the late order of government has been removed from the public crossways, and now hangs up, as a memento of God's wonderful doings, in this Christian parlor. Yes, 'God reigns!' 'Let the earth rejoice!' 'None that ever put their trust in him shall be ashamed.' 'In the Lord Jehovah is everlasting strength.' Am I not right in feeling as in the presence of the wonder-working God in view of these things?

"Then I wish to note the decided Christian character of the house. Here are illuminated texts beautifying the walls, and speaking of 'Faith, Hope, and

Charity,' of ' God is my salvation,' and giving 'Glory to God in the highest,' and on earth proclaiming ' Peace and good-will to men.' Here in every room hang hymns, texts, and daily promises; Christian works of practical piety lie side by side with those of science. This is as it ought to be, but alas! is seldom found elsewhere.

"September 3.

"I should close my letter before leaving this delightful home, but as it is now late, and I must start at dawn, it will be impossible to say all I could wish. Yesterday and today we spent in visiting scenes of interest in the locality, including the famous temples and the tomb of Ieasu, situated seven miles from here, on the sea-shore facing the Pacific, and located high up on a mountain - a flight of stone steps twelve feet wide winding up across the face of the lofty bluff, with hand railings of massive masonry. The temple where he is worshipped and the tomb itself are of wonderful workmanship.

"A lofty five-story tower has just been sold by order of government, and removed, although it was the crowning glory of this sublime mausoleum. This is owing to the tower being an emblem of Buddhism, and the government is trying to do away with it in favor of Shintoism. Ieasu had been a great patron of Buddhism. Its priests had given him aid in war, and he rewarded them in peace by making Buddhism the state religion.

"The removal of his dynasty, together with the system he established, is again the wonderful work of God. Mr. Clark tried hard to purchase material enough of the tower to make the pulpit of the first native Christian church in Japan. They were eager to sell, but finding we wanted it much they went up proportionately on the price.

"This afternoon I spent a couple of hours in the laboratory connected with the school. Here, too, were the walls illuminated with Scriptural and other appropriate texts. Over the clock and over the door was ' God bless our school,' supported by ' Prove all things, hold fast that which is good,' ' Let not your heart be troubled,' ' Peace I leave with you,' 'Speak the truth,' etc. Maps of the United States, presented by Commodore Perry twenty years ago, grace the

walls. Rare works fill the library. Two immense Holland atlases of over one hundred years old show all parts of the then known world with a remarkable fidelity. All the maps had names written in Chinese characters on gilt paper, and pasted over the countries, showing that they had been carefully preserved for the Tycoon's use.

"The opening hours of school exercises were spent in singing 'Just as I am,' ' I was a wandering sheep,' ' joyfully, joyfully,' ' From all that dwell,' and numerous other Sunday school hymns. The boys first repeated the verses from memory with great ease and propriety. They sang well, Brother Clark playing the organ and leading them. The long-meter doxology was on the blackboard. It was their last exercise in closing. I gave them a Japanese translation of it, which I had made for our own use in Yokohama, and they sang it at once, and, seemed pleased with it, the first time I presume they have ever heard God's praise attempted in the Japanese language."

Chapter Five

Excursions and Comical Experiences

The sights and scenery of a country can best be studied by roaming around on foot, and going to out-of-the-way places where primitive customs prevail, and where nature has had full play. Occasionally I would take a holiday and tramp off among the mountains, or go on hunting expeditions through districts never before visited by a foreigner. At other times I would be sent for to make some scientific researches in a neighboring province, where black stones suggested the proximity of coal, or shining fragments of iron or copper pyrites were kindled, by the Japanese imagination, into hidden mines of gold. "All is not gold that glitters," would be my usual response to the yellow missiles sent to me for analysis.

71

Sometimes I was sent for to vaccinate a baby. Smallpox is very prevalent in Japan, and I was supposed to be equal to every emergency, whether to vaccinate a baby, find a coal mine, teach a school, build a house, or measure a mountain.

One day in July I started off on an excursion with a party of my students to visit a famous waterfall thirty miles distant, located in the region south-west of Fujiyama. I knew the young men needed exercise, for they studied too hard and walked too little; so I planned that we should make the tour on foot after leaving the high-road, and I knew that no kind of conveyance's could be obtained there for such as were inclined to be lazy.

We got along very well until the latter part of the afternoon, when, after traversing a great tea district, and resting at the ruins of an ancient Buddhist temple, one of the most beautiful I ever saw, we entered the rolling and hilly region leading towards the magnificent slope of the "Matchless Mountain." Here we were overtaken by a storm, and the wind and rain nearly drenched the romance out of us. We entered the woods and made our way as fast as the steep and slippery nature of the ground would admit, hoping to arrive at some habitation where we might rest and spend a comfortable night. The waterfall was only three miles away, but as the rain was too much for us we decided to put off visiting it until next morning. The whole region abounded in rapid streams and miniature cataracts, and as we trudged along, we could hear the thumping of a Japanese waterwheel turning on its rude axle and driving a heavy wooden hammer by means of projecting spokes, which pounded the rice into powder. Usually the rice is pounded into flour in the way shown in the accompanying illustration, where a man stands all day in the sun and pounds the rice in a wooden mortar with a large wooden hammer. It is very hard work, but he gets used to it, and simply stops now and then to wipe the perspiration from his naked body. The man in the picture has as much clothing upon him as most of the country people wear in the summer.

We passed Japanese farmers "ploughing" in the field. One man guided the plough, while another led the horse. But the men, the horse, and the plough were all in two feet of water and mud, and presented a ridiculous appearance as they rushed back and forth in the miry field, with the rain pouring upon them, and with only straw hats and straw coverings over their bodies. When the rice field is stirred up into a perfect mush of mud, they consider it fit for planting.

At last we arrived at a thatched-roof farmhouse, which our guide said was the best place in that neighborhood for us to spend the night. But the two old women of the house did not welcome us very warmly, and said they had nothing for us to eat, and no good place for us to sleep. We were not going to be driven out again into the rain and cold, however, so we said we would manage to get along, and told the old folks to get a hot bath ready and then give us some supper. I was wet to the skin when I arrived at these uncomfortable quarters, and as there was not a thing for me to put on, I knew I must catch a severe cold unless I could manage to get my clothes dry. So I told them to build a good fire, and then said I would get into the hot bath and wait patiently till one of the students dried my clothes. Their bathing arrangements were of a decidedly primitive order; nevertheless, I had to make the best of the circumstances. The bathtub was a round wooden concern, with a little copper oven placed in its side, and in this oven a little fire was built, so that the person bathing and the fire itself are literally in the bath together! This big tub stood - not in some private corner, as you would imagine, but directly in the center of the house, and in the most conspicuous place, close to the entrance door. Grouped about it were the women and children, all waiting for the fun of seeing the Tojin get into his bath! But modesty is at a discount in this part of the world, and I could not stand shivering in the cold while my wet clothes were drying; so after one or two futile attempts to drive the spectators away, I made a bold dash and succeeded in submerging myself in the scalding contents of the tub!

Here I thought I would be at ease for awhile but I found as I reached the bottom of the tub that the mud of the region was by no means confined to their rice fields, for such a slimy tub I never had the misfortune to be in before, and I wanted to get out immediately. Besides, the water smelled as though they had been boiling old fish in it, and if I turned about now and then to get a fresh sniff of air, I was sure to strike my legs against that hot copper oven with the fire a it! Then I would give a jump, but as I appeared above the rim of the tub a dozen eyes would be fixed upon me to see what was the matter. Now and then a farmer or neighbor would come in at the door, and be transfixed with astonishment at the strange apparition, which greeted him in the tub. Not that the sight of cuticle was by any means new to him, but such a chalky creature as the one before him had never appeared in his zoological experience; and many of the farmers rubbed their eyes, as they came in and out, to see whether it were a ghost or not.

At last, the clothes were dry, and I arose from the tub a little wiser, if not cleaner, from the operation. But hardly had I stepped out of the water before another person stepped in, and when he was through still another followed, till I counted during the evening at least a dozen different individuals who bathed in that same tub, and in the same water, one right after another!

The next thing on the program was supper; but supper they had none to give us, and this was not the most agreeable information, inasmuch as we were cold and hungry, and had walked fifteen miles without any thing to eat. We also knew that we must walk the same distance next day, and it was necessary for us to get something substantial with which to build up our energies. One of the students proposed therefore to the old farmer, when he came in, that he should kill a chicken and make soup for us. But the old fellow shook his head in horror at the very idea of it, and whispered that it was well known to all the people of the region thereabouts that whosoever killed a fowl would have his house destroyed by the gods, and he besought us not to ever speak of such a thing lest destruction should be brought upon him. Neither could he be prevailed upon at first even to cook some eggs for us; but we tried to prove to him that eggs were not chickens, so at last he yielded, but said we must not *eat* them!

After a scanty supper of eggs and rice, and the poorest tea that ever was put over a fire, we prepared ourselves for bed. But going to bed in Japan is rather an indefinite expression for any one accustomed to sleep between sheets and comforters and upon snowy pillows. In fact you do not "go" to the bed at all, but the bed, such as it is, simply *comes* to you; and the style of preparing for the night is about the same wherever you are. First, a cotton-stuffed mat is laid anywhere upon the floor, and a block or roll is placed at one end to rest (?) your head upon. Then you lie down, and a cotton-stuffed quilt is thrown over you.

This quilt is like a Jap dress on a big scale, with large and heavily stuffed sleeves, which flap over you like wings. But the difficulty is that these capacious sleeves, with all the rest of the bedding, contain unnumbered legions of voracious fleas hid away in recesses known only to themselves, but which only wait till you get fairly nestled in sleep when they begin their onslaught on their defenseless and helpless victims. Awakened by the merciless havoc they are making upon you, it is in vain that you roll and toss and shake your clothes till you are wearied out; that only increases the vigor with which they renew the battle, and though you may spend hours in the faint glare of the primitive oil lantern, which is set in one corner of the room, and strive to rid yourself of the tiny tigers that are devouring you, it is all to no purpose, and you sink down at last asleep. But you are soon awakened again, only to undergo the same tribulation, and the long hours of night pass away as you pace up and down the narrow limits of the room listening to the snoring of the dozen or more tough-hided sleepers who surround you, and peep through the sliding shutters of the house to see if day is breaking or not. You cannot lie down again, for the floor is crawling with the creatures you dread, and you cannot *sit* down, for there is nothing to sit upon, and such a thing as a chair was never heard of in that region; neither can you take even a sniff of fresh air on the balcony, for the house is boxed up entirely with the windowless and doorless sliding- shutters, which you strive in vain to force open. Besides, the rain pours in torrents outside, and you would only be drenched in any attempt to change the situation. Such was the miserable and tiresome night I passed after the day's fatigue, which preceded it. The morning found me sleepless, tired, and hungry, and with scarcely a square, inch of my body, which was not covered with bites innumerable. The rain was still pouring outside, and our prospects for the day were not very cheerful. Nevertheless we laughed at our misfortunes, and began tramping off again over the hills, though it was with difficulty we could keep our feet, for the paths were steep and slippery, and the wind blew the rain in our faces till we were half blind. We were bound to get to the waterfall, which we had set out to see, though we had hardly reckoned upon such an abundant "waterfall" as that through which we were now passing.

As we drew near, the roar of many waters greeted us, and the sound grew louder and deeper as we passed under the dripping foliage and descended the precipitous and rocky path which led us to the bottom of a wild, romantic-looking canyon, completely shut in by steep rocky walls nearly a hundred feet high. The main waterfall was situated at the innermost end of the circular-shaped gorge in which we stood, and though its height was not more than sixty or seventy feet it was very beautiful. The amount of water was considerable, and it fell in one solid column, which struck with great force in the oval basin below. The noise was almost deafening, because the sounds reverberated from the walls of the gorge, which encircled us with a circumference of not more than five hundred feet. The Japs call this fall the great "White Rope," and the little fall close to it they call "Silver Threads," because there are so many of them spinning down over the rocks. The main fall reminded me somewhat of the *Staubbach* in Switzerland, for there are surely a thousand miniature fountains which leap from the rocky precipice to the right of the main fall, and these add greatly to the beauty and romance of the scene just to the left, also, there is a "Bridal Veil" fall - thin, smooth, and transparent in its airy descent. There is a rich border of foliage enclosing the whole gorge, and setting off the falls, the foam, and the cataracts to great advantage. It is, on the whole, the prettiest spot I have seen in Japan.

The ex-Tycoon lived not far from my house, near a temple founded by his illustrious ancestors. He was very fond of hunting and hawking, and as I wanted to make his acquaintance and see his trained hawks, I sent him a pretty chromo of a hunting scene and invited him to take tea with me. He replied very politely in an elegant perfumed note, written with his own hand, saying that he wanted to come and see me in my new house, but that political difficulties were in the way, for he was an exile. He thanked me for the invitation, and for kindness in teaching his people; and as a slight token of his regard sent me an immense aquarium bowl made of the finest Chinaware, and carried by four men. The bowl was beautifully ornamented with blue waves, fishes, and turtles, and was so large that I sat in it and had my photograph taken! "Sam Patch" attempted to extemporize a bath-tub out of this bowl one day by putting several gallons of hot water in it, when it exploded with a terrific noise, frightening the wits out of poor Sam, and leaving me only fragments of my present from the Tycoon!

Not succeeding in securing a hawk hunt with the Tycoon, I started off on a grand boar hunt in a wild mountainous section of the country, where no foreigner had ever penetrated before. I left the students behind this time, as they could not stand the fatigue, and took my most reliable guard with me. The governors of the province gave me guides, and ordered nearly two hundred armed men of that section to go with me and beat up the game.

When I reached the neighborhood of the hunting ground, I found myself at the head of a small army of wild-looking Japanese farmers, who carried old-fashioned guns, which they fired with a slow match. They had never seen a foreigner and gazed at me with as much curiosity as I did at them and their queer guns.

On arriving at the hunting ground, we discovered several deer standing under a tree on top of the bill. The men divided into three parties and soon surrounded the three ravines in which the hunt was to take place, and through which they were to beat along in the underbrush, driving the game before them. I stood on a low cliff, at the base of which the ravines converged, and shot at the game started from the bush when I could do so without endangering the men below. The hunters were all hidden in the underbrush and tall grass, but the noise they made was frightful; they yelled like demons, and fired their guns incessantly, while the dogs kept barking furiously as the unseen but noisy circle closed slowly upon the game within the three ravines.

Now and then a wild boar would dash out and attempt to break through the line of fire by rushing headlong up the hill. Fifty balls would follow him before he reached ten paces, and, if he were not killed outright, the dogs would dash after him; but the dogs sometimes had the worst of it if they happened near his sharp tusks while he was yet alive. The frightened deer were driven down the glade and died without a struggle.

At noon all of the men came together on the side of the hill and ate balls of boiled rice, which they carried, in small boxes. This they considered a satisfactory dinner; each ball weighed half a pound and had a plum or raisin inside of it. They looked at my cake, crackers, and bread and butter with great wonder. After dinner, I made them fire a salute of two hundred guns, to hear the marvelous echo of the valley and to end the day's sport.

They brought up three wild boars and two fine deer, which they laid at my feet, and I said this was sufficient to supply me with fresh meat for some time. The largest boar weighed nearly two hundred pounds, and was a fierce-looking fellow it required eight men to carry him to the city.

Subsequently I sent my friends and the governors steaks of venison and slices of fresh pork; while at home I had the first roast meats that I had enjoyed for many months.

In a duck hunt shortly after this, which I had in another section of the country, I was not quite so fortunate in finding the people friendly. I did not know that the feeling against foreigners was so bitter there until I had rather dangerous proof of it. A small lake nestling among the hills had been a resort for thousands of wild ducks for a long time. The sound of a gun had never been heard there, for it was prohibited, and the people of the village near by caught the ducks now and then in nets. The day that I went there the governors gave the people permission to use their guns and hunt with me. They cast very savage looks at me, for they hated foreigners.

When I reached the lake small ambuscades had been constructed of bushes and boughs of trees along the shore, and the surface of the water was literally covered with ducks "so wild that they were tame." As the first volley of shot echoed among the hills a myriad of quacking creatures rose in a great cloud from the surface of the lake and wheeled over our heads in frightened confusion. The sky was darkened with the feathered fugitives, and the noise made by their wings was like a mighty, rushing wind. Flock after flock swept in graceful curves through the air just above us, their white breasts flashing for a moment in the sun, and their wings in such rapid motion that trey fanned our faces as they flew past and settled again slowly upon the surface of the water.

The lake had always been their quiet home, and they knew not whither to flee; besides, their enemies were completely hidden by the thick ambuscades. Another volley soon started them again, and they rose in the air leaving many of their dead and wounded companions upon the surface of the lake. Now their flight became swift and broken, and as they passed close above our heads we fired indiscriminately into their midst, causing the flocks to scatter in frightened confusion. Down they came at last upon the death-laden surface of the water, and so tired were they that they simply ducked their heads as shot after shot skipped along beside them. The firing continued the whole morning, until some of the flocks had retreated to a neighboring lake and the sportsmen were contented with the fruits of the slaughter.

At this juncture, I was standing on the further margin of the lake leaning on my gun, my guard having left me for a few minutes, when I heard a peculiar whir close to my head. Thinking it was a duck, I turned suddenly and saw the bullet had struck the bank beside me, spattering me with mud. On looking in the direction from which the shot came, I discovered a Japanese in full flight with his weapon trailing behind him. I knew that he had fired at me, for there were no ducks near at the time, and as the fellow was not yet out of range I raised my gun to reciprocate the compliment.

Shimojo, my interpreter, was near by, and I said to him, "Shall I shoot?" "Yes," he said, "for he fired at you; but we must not hope to escape, for they will kill us." "Then discretion is the better part of valor, "I replied; "for as he missed me, I think we had better not punish him."

I lowered my gun and went to the other part of the lake, where a dense grove skirted the shore. Here I stationed myself near a tree, when whir! came another shot, skipping across the narrow arm of the lake and striking the ground near me; again another came, and I saw my guard lay down his gun and run to the water's edge. A boy who was standing near by had been shot in the calf of the leg, and though we washed the wound and sent him to the hospital at Shidzuoka, he died a day or two after.

In returning from the lake we happened into a perfect nest of smallpox, which I feared more than the Japanese swords or bullets; but fortunately none of us caught the contagion. The people of Todomi, a province thirty miles south of my own, found a large hill with oil trickling down its side, and sent some of it to me for examination. I found it very good petroleum oil, and sent them several of its products obtained by distillation; they were very much pleased, and wanted to dig deep wells. The governors of the province requested me to come to the oil district and tell the people where to dig. Accordingly I started off at half-past four one morning, and tried to get on the journey before the heat of the day came on. Most of the distance we went in kangos, so that our progress was slow. It makes one feel like a monkey in a cage to be carried all over the country in one of these bamboo baskets slung upon a stick, and having people stare at you as if you belonged to a traveling menagerie. However, I soon became used to it.

We were delayed in crossing the rocky channel of a very wide river where the current was swift, and our flatboat, propelled by bamboo poles, nearly upset us in the stream. The country through which we passed abounded in large snakes; they crossed our path repeatedly, and one black fellow, six feet long, coiled up on a footbridge and would not let the coolies pass. One of my bearers poked him gently with a stick, whereupon his snakeship moved slowly away into the marsh.

On arriving at the village I inspected the oil district carefully, and then selected the spot where I thought they ought to dig. Subsequently they sunk an artesian well, and struck oil in great abundance.

Before daybreak the next morning, I was on my way back to Shidzuoka. Early as it was, the yaconims, or officials of the village, escorted us with gaily-painted lanterns to the end of their district, and then squatted on the ground, bowing their beads and heaving such deep sighs of respect that we almost regretted leaving them.

We were now passing along the seashore, and the early morning scene was perfectly enchanting. The gray mist still hung upon the face of the water, and the air was so peaceful that scarcely a wave rippled the surface of the ocean. Soon the sun rose. At first only a rim of light was to be seen slowly rising from the Pacific, then it began to glow into a great dome of fire, and finally the whole round orb was seen floating in the mist like a fairy world.

A few months afterwards a delegation of old men came to see me from the oil province, to thank me for going there, and to report that they were getting several hundred gallons of oil daily. These old men were dressed in the old-fashioned style, never having seen any foreign innovations, and I thought I would impress them with the wonders of the outer world by taking them into my laboratory. They looked in great astonishment at the performances of the electric machines, air-pump, steam-engine, and the model of a small sawmill which I had just constructed; but what excited their interest more than any thing else was a small toy wagon wound up by clock-work, which had recently been sent to me from America as a present to a young Japanese. This wagon I wound up without their knowing it, and placed it under an inverted tub in the middle of the room; then I asked one of the old men to lift up the tub. Away went the tin horses and wagon, prancing around the room before the astonished eyes of the old men, until, after making several complete circuits, and doing, apparently, whatever I told them, the tin horses stopped at my feet. The old men looked at each other in wondering silence a few minutes, and then said they didn't know "whether those painted horses were pulling the wagon, or the wagon was pushing the horses!"

They went home to dine with me, when their surprise was still more augmented at the strange things to eat; and they returned to their province saying that it would take the rest of their lives to tell the wonders they had seen.

My scientific experiments were a constant source of delight to the Japanese, for they are fond of any thing practical; and although my students understood the laws and principles concerned, the common people were bewildered and amazed. I gave a series of experiments one-day in my lecture-room before the governors of the province and a large number of people who came in from mere curiosity. I wanted to show the officials my model sawmill, having a small circular saw run by a diminutive steam-engine. I told them it was a pity to see dozens of men and boys with long handsaws sweltering and working the whole day in sawing boards from a single log, as I had seen them do in building my house, when a modern sawmill could perform ten times the amount of work in half the time. They watched my little machine as it cut rapidly through small sticks of wood, and then said it was very wonderful; but, if they were to establish such a sawmill in Shidzuoka, it would be mobbed or raise a riot among the workmen.

I never witnessed a more ludicrous sight than the effects produced upon the Japanese by some of my experiments. The innocent manner in which they stepped up to the various electric machines, and did whatever they were told, was only excelled by the dumb astonishment or the frantic yell with which they received the electric shock. No visible effect, however great, upon the first who wanted to take hold was sufficient to restrain the intense curiosity of those who wished to follow. They wanted to feel for themselves, and their ambition was usually satisfied after one trial.

Two of the governors took a "spark" from one of the machines, but the third was very dignified and would not deign to come up to the table, as it was contrary to strict etiquette. So I politely offered to bring him some electricity in a bottle. He doubted whether that could be done. In order to dispel his doubts, and also to bring him down to the level of ordinary mortals, I took a large Leyden jar, which I charged full of electricity, and brought it to him with good grace. He looked at the jar, and seeing nothing in it concluded to touch the brass knob at the top. The effect may be better imagined than described, only he didn't show any more dignity or touch any more jars that day!

There were a number of Samurai gentry on the back seats, who do not like foreigners very well, but who looked on very wisely, as though they understood every thing that was going on.

As they declined to come up to the table like the other people, or to touch any of the instruments, I thought I would close the entertainment by sending them a few electrical compliments.

At my request they all joined hands with great glee, thinking they were too far away to get hurt. I then connected my large Ruhmkorff's coil, which is a very powerful machine, with a battery bidden in the closet, and took the long wires to the Samurai gentlemen at either end of the line. They innocently took the wires, and the next moment I touched the key of the coil, and sent them an electric shock, which tumbled the whole of them over among the benches!

The Japanese musicians of Shidzuoka favored me with several "concerts," which were as marvelous to me as some of my performances were to them. Their instruments were well made, but very curious. They were mostly stringed instruments, fifes, and drums.

Seating themselves upon the floor, the musicians would play together, making a chaos of sound beyond description. It seemed like a chorus of wild animals suddenly let loose. I could not keep from laughing, although I wanted to appear polite. There was no "tune" to the music, and when they attempted to sing the effect was rather monotonous.

After the "concert" I gave the musicians a supper, which they enjoyed, showing their appreciation of the good things by filling their sleeves with them to take home to their families. This is the Japanese custom, and they think it very proper. The musicians were pleased with my melodeon; they wanted to know where the music came from, for they could not see any strings.

Chapter 6

The Ascent Of Fuji-Yama.

The Japanese have an old legend, that their magnificent mountain Fuji-Yama rose from the earth in a single night, and at the same time a great depression formed in a distant province, which filled with water and became the beautiful Lake Biwa. The mountain has always been held in superstitious reverence, and the people perform pilgrimages of hundreds of miles that they may stand and worship upon the sacred summit.

Early in the spring, when the snow has melted on the mountain, the ascent is comparatively safe, and several days are usually allowed for the undertaking. Later in the year, as winter approaches, the mountain becomes well nigh inaccessible. Its cone-shaped peak is shrouded in snow during ten months of the year, and fleecy clouds are continually chasing each other around the icy slope, or piling themselves in a peculiar pyramidal form on the mountaintop. Sometimes, when the sky is perfectly cloudless elsewhere, a cap, curved like a dome, and formed from a single white cloud, will rest for hours upon the head of Fuji, crowning the sacred mountain with additional glory, and presenting a picture of Surpassing beauty, as the snowy peak and the white cloud appear against the deep-blue background of the sky.

Fuji-Yama rises from the midst of an immense plain, and though smaller mountain ranges are seen on all sides, it stands absolutely alone in the grandeur of its proportions. Its summit is visible a hundred miles away, and the Japanese have constructed a large map of thirteen provinces, from each of which the top may be seen. The view presented in the accompanying picture is taken twenty miles from the mountain; in the foreground are a few farm hovels, and a small stream used in irrigating the rice-fields, which are always kept under water.

Since arriving in Japan it had been my constant ambition to make the ascent of the "Matchless Mountain;" but circumstances did not favor the attempt until the second year of my sojourn in Shidsuoka. Even then I was unable, owing to my duties, to select the proper season when pilgrimages are made, but was obliged to assail the mountain in the midst of storms, and under every possible disadvantage.

The first attempt was a failure, and I was forced to retreat after spending two days and nights in a terrible storm on the side of the mountain. The second attempt was successful, and I reached the summit and measured the height; but again I was caught in storms and again obliged to retreat. Both of these experiences, severe as they were, gave me a very satisfactory idea of the mountain and its surroundings. The first attempt was made on the north side, in company with my friend Rev. Mr. Ballagh, previous to his visit to my home in Shidzuoka; the second attempt was made on the south side.

Mr. Ballagh and I left Yokohama together, and traveled two days through an open region of country, leaving the usual route of the Tokaido and crossing three mountain ranges; we then passed a broad lava plain which brought us to the base of Fuji-Yama. The second day we rose by starlight, and started off, mounted upon a pair of Japanese pack- horses. These packhorses have huge contrivances fixed on their backs, which are grotesquely called saddles; upon these the baggage and sacks of food for the horse are placed, and firmly attached by ropes. You are then made to scramble to the top of it all as best you may be able; and it is much like being perched on the bump of a dromedary thus to ride on the back of a frisky Japanese horse, who only awaits his chance of upsetting you from your exalted position. A Japanese leads the horse by a loose rope halter; as straw-shod animal picks his uneven way some steep road or over some rocky mountain pass, you take your uncertain chance of either spinning over his head or sliding over his tail. If you happen to meet a few other quadrupeds of like persuasion, there immediately ensues a complimentary interchange of heels and hoofs and neighs, that in no wise improves the situation.

The Hakone range of mountains was on our left, and before us stood the dark and clouded Oyama range, where a dread deity is said to reside; the highest peak of this range is visited by throngs of pilgrims, who worship at the shrine, and seek exemption from dreaded evils, which this frowning deity is wont to send upon mankind. Early in the morning, before daylight had dawned, we heard the tinkling bells and deep-toned gongs preceding the mournful worship on this mountain.

We crossed a river in the afternoon, where fine fish are caught by means of a *live* fish, which the Japanese put on the end of a line, and thereby entice other fish of the same kind and of gregarious disposition into nets prepared for their reception.

We took dinner at a wayside hotel, where we had good accommodations and an hour's rest, and on taking leave our host presented his bill to the fabulous extent of two cents and a half! The districts through which we passed were given over to the cultivation of the tobacco plant, which thrives here well, and its broad leaves were spreading out in every direction. The sugarcane fields were also very numerous, and looked like fields of corn twelve feet high.

Towards evening all vegetation was left behind, and we entered one of the most barren and desolate tracts of country I ever saw anywhere. It was nothing more nor less than one great series of lava-beds, and the soil was like packed coal-dust, without any object to direct us.

Before long, we lost our way, and where to go or what to do we did not know. The night was as dark as pitch, and not a star could be seen, while dark and heavy clouds covered the sky. The earth on which we trod was blacker than the sky above us, and at every step the crispy lava crumbled under our feet. The only way in which we could pick our path through this trackless waste was by *watching for old straw shoes,* which had been left upon the wayside by pilgrims gone before.

Although the country was level, yet there was absolutely nothing to be seen in any direction. Neither light nor lantern glimmered from afar, to guide us even to some lone hut or hovel, where a human being could be found to tell us where we were. Everything was as still as death, and not a sound nor sight was there to show that we were in even remote proximity to a living thing. Not a cultivated spot did we meet for miles, and neither tree nor shrub was to be seen.

At last, we came to a dead stop, for we had on more elevated ground, and a small river was heard tumbling through a gully near us. The two Japs who were leading our horses knew as little about this part of the country as we did; however, they searched over the black fields with a little paper lantern, and ere long one of them struck upon a path. Following this, we passed through some low brushwood, and, turning the point of a dark knoll, suddenly found ourselves at the entrance of a village. This proved to be the place we were seeking, and, tired and hungry, we rode down through the long street, where the people must have taken us for ghosts; we had found it so cold on the lava plains that I had wrapped myself in two large sheets, they being the only available things I had with me, and consequently I looked like a mounted specter in from the wilderness.

When it was known that we were not ghosts but foreigners, we were asked if we would like to put up at a temple; and the offer was eagerly accepted, for both of us had once lived in temples, and we knew we should feel quite at home. So our horses were led into a secluded place among tall trees, where we dismounted, and tumbled in haste through the front door of the temple. We found things looking quite hospitable inside, and were delighted at the prospect of getting good rest and sleep.

The old idol was sitting in the Middle of the place, in rather gloomy silence, as though he didn't like the idea of his sacred abode being made a wayside tavern for *Tojins,* or foreigners; but we didn't mind what he thought about it, but passed along to the table and chairs which bad been provided for us. Here we had steaming pea soup soon placed before us, the savor of which must have been enough to rouse our bronze idol friend from his lethargy, had he been susceptible to anything better than the incense usually burnt before him. The priests were very polite and accommodating, and supplied our wants as well as they could. After a good supper we stretched ourselves upon the clean straw mats, and were soon sound asleep. Our sleep didn't last long, for at midnight I was awakened by a general commotion at the temple, and amid the glimmer of lanterns I saw a pair of foreign boots stride into the heard a whistle of "Johnny comes marching home," and then a few loud orders in plain Saxon that there was no mistaking.

Half asleep as I was, I wondered if Mr. Ballagh had got up in a nightmare; but feeling around on the floor I soon found he was still asleep. My torch, however awakened him, and we found that two other foreigners had arrived, and that they (with about a dozen coolies) were about to themselves as comfortable as circumstances would permit.

We were in no very amiable mood at thus being roused from our sleep; and finding that we were not able to secure as quiet a night as we hoped, we arose and prepared ham and eggs for breakfast at three o'clock, with pineapple for dessert, and ordered the horses we started off again in the dark.

The real assent of Fuji-Yama now began, and passing a temple to the right - dedicated to the god of the mountain - we entered a broad avenue leading up the slope, and shut in on either side by a low and spare growth of sickly-looking pines. For nearly six miles there was little of interest to notice. The ground was easy to walk upon, being composed of the same black ashy deposit of lava which we met in the dismal plains below, and which reminded me of soft coal granulated to the size of large peas.

As the daylight came slowly on, we could see that the clouds were thickening about us, instead of diminishing, and that the mist and drizzle were changing to a regular storm of rain. However, we pushed on to the station, which we knew to be a little ahead, and just as the weather was getting the better of us we arrived at two old dilapidated straw shanties, where we set to work to make ourselves as much at home as possible.

As this was the station beyond which horses were not able to go, we had our goods unpacked and sent the horses away, retaining two coolies with us to carry things and make themselves generally useful. A small fire was burning on the floor of the shanty, and a forlorn-looking Jap had a scanty kettle of rice simmering over the embers. We piled on plenty of wood, and got ourselves well dried, and then spreading a straw mat and plenty of newspapers on the ground, we lay down and went to sleep. After a few hours we got up, and attempted to take observations on the situation; but as we were still in the midst of clouds and mist, we could see nothing, and the rain continued to pour worse than ever.

At this juncture the two foreigners suddenly made their appearance, whom we had left snoozing some hours before at the base of the mountain. "Misery loves company;" so we greeted them their wet garments, and put more sticks on the fire to give them a warm welcome. They were glad enough to avail themselves of the primitive hospitality offered, and after seating themselves on two empty washtubs, formally introduced themselves as " Mr. T—, of San Franciso" and "Doctor X—, of New Zealand." Before long we all held a council of war as to whether we were to attempt storming the heights of Fuji-Yama on that day or not. Some of us were in favor of pushing on, in hopes of rising *above* the clouds and out of reach of the storm. But one or two rain-soaked pilgrims, who came the mountain just then, reported squalls of wind and rain near the summit, we were forced to the unanimous conclusion that there was no mountain-climbing in store for us on that day at least.

We spent the day in reading, talking, and sleeping; and our English friend from New Zealand gave us no little information concerning the condition of affairs down there - where we usually consider things rather topsy-turvy, but where, judging from his account, they are decidedly right side up, progressive and hopeful. We were not lacking in canned provisions, so that we managed to get along quite comfortably notwithstanding the limited accommodations for cooking.

Towards evening I explored the other shanty situated just below us, and though apparently intended for horses, I concluded it would serve a better purpose for our camping out overnight than the more fragile structure in which we were then stowed away. Its roof did not leak so badly, and it had a large fireplace on the ground, where we could keep up a rousing fire all night, and defy both wind, cold, and rain.

So we made the coolies collect large logs and piles of wood, and after making substantial seats to sleep upon, we took our traps and occupied our new quarters, leaving the coolies to get along as best they could in the other shanty. We also boarded up our new establishment on three sides, for it never had any walls, as it was merely a straw roof supported on wooden posts. Here we felt quite in luxury; and as darkness came on and the storm increased we had a fire roaring and crackling away, which threatened at times to burn up our shanty and all that it contained.

But even in this elevated region our merciless foes, the fleas, did not cease from persecuting us; and in order to be rid of them I climbed up on top of some long poles, which were stretched across the garret part of the roof, and finding a bundle of straw reeds there, I unrolled it, got inside, and went to sleep. It was rather an uncertain roost to slumber upon, for the poles were a foot or so apart, and if I should unconsciously roll over or turn around lengthwise, I would surely go through.

Waking up now and then during the night, it was a curious scene to look down from my shaky perch to the spot where the campfire was burning brightly. There lay two or three sleepers stretched upon boards, and covered with all sorts of things imaginable; and once in a while a ghostly form would be seen moving stealthily around the fire poking the embers. The rain was driving in sheets against our frail habitation, and howled mournfully about us. It was to roost up on my pole berth for any length of time, even though the wind occasionally sent me a blast of hot air and smoke from the fire; so every half hour I took to the ladder and went down to warm myself, and to put on more wood.

We had a Robinson Crusoe experience of it that night, and in the morning the storm had not abated in the least, but the rain came down in torrents, as though the supply above was inexhaustible. We saw it was no use hoping any longer, and now whether to march down the mountain again, was the question. Two pilgrims, passing by in a sorry plight, reported a still more doleful condition of things above, so we gloomily wrapped ourselves up in large sheets of Jap oil-paper, and prepared to descend. I had half a dozen copies of *Harper's Weekly* bound tightly about my legs, which gave me quite a pictorial appearance; and when fairly fixed, we started on a trot down the slope, leaving the coolies to follow with the baggage. The wind came in gusts that nearly took us off our feet, and the rain was blinding, so that we could scarcely see our way. But we made good time, and after an hour of thorough drenching we arrived at our temple hotel, wiser if not better men.

Not succeeding in getting *over* the mountain, we had to manage to get *around* it. So we soon started off again through the rain, some in kangos and some on horseback, and after six hours traveling we arrived at a village on the Tokaido, from which the ascent of the southern side of the Halcone' Pass is made. When we came to the river Fusi-kawa, it was so swollen by the recent heavy rains as to be utterly impassable for boats. We therefore saw that we must experience another check, and settled down to our fate as best we could. However, it turned out better than we anticipated.

Just as we were starting out to look at the impetuous river, whom should we meet but my interpreter, whom I had previously sent ahead with provisions and supplies from Yokohama. He, too, had been stopped by the freshet, so we found all our boxes and baggage, and could afford to laugh at our empty lunch-basket and travel-soiled clothes; now we had provisions to stand a siege, and clean clothing enough to dress like daimios, or princes. So we made merry over our misfortune, and secured airy rooms in a quiet place, and fixed ourselves up for a sojourn over Sunday, expecting on the first of the week to start on our way again. Here at Yoshiwara, where we had to pass the Sabbath, Mr. Ballagh had two or three preachings during the day; and indeed everywhere we went, with inimitable tact and zeal, he scattered gospel truth. It was delightful to see how much good could be done on a simple jaunt of needed recreation, by one intent upon improving, or making, opportunities of speaking for the Master.

Although baffled in this first attempt to ascend Fuji-Yama, I by no means gave up, but kept watching from a distance, waiting to renew the effort whenever the clouds were fairly lifted. But it was late in the season, and the rainy weather had set in, so that it was not till the middle of September that a real bright day made its appearance. However, on the sixteenth it was a glorious day, and a holiday at that, being the festival of the Mikado's divine descent, and also the day of my leaving Albany for Japan just two years before; so off I started for Fuji-Yama, with the wild hope of finding myself at its summit within twenty-four hours of leaving Shidz-u-o-ka. This feat was really accomplished, but I never want to try it again!

I left home in the afternoon, reaching the river-crossing at Fusi-kawa about dusk. Passing over in a boat, I left the Tokaido, and struck across the country to Omiya, six miles distant. I had with me a guide and a Japanese student, whose pedestrian powers were not very promising. Arriving at the village, we put up at the house of the principal person of the place, who was a friend of ours and entertained us very kindly. I could not sleep

though; and having ordered three horses early, we started off again at precisely two o'clock, hoping to get well up the lower slope, or base, of the
mountain before daylight. This early morning ride was one of the most
charming I ever enjoyed; and even the severe fatigue which succeeded it
could not detract from its romance and beauty. The night was perfectly
clear, and cool enough to make one's overcoat comfortable; scarcely a
cloud bigger than one's hand could be seen, and the new moon with its
pale crescent was just rising as we set out. The dark outline of the mountain was before us, apparently so near that one might touch it; yet we had
to go just twelve in miles before fairly reaching its base, and then ten miles
more (as the Japanese call it) ere reaching the top.

After riding two hours, we came to Mori-yama, the last habitable place to
be met with. Here our road became a mere bridle-path, and entered a region
entirely destitute of cultivation. Though this slope of country was not cultivated, owing to its elevation, yet it was far from presenting the dreary aspect
of the section similarly situated on the northern side of the mountain, which
I had traversed a few weeks before. Instead of black lava fields covering the
earth like a pall, there was a broad stretch of land covered with long rank
grass, presenting an appearance not unlike some of our Western prairies at
home. As we came up higher, the surface became more undulating, and
ridges had to be crossed. It felt homelike up in this region; for the landscape
at times had quite a New England look, and was suggestive of many pleasant associations. As the sun rose, and threw its fresh morning glow over it
all, the birds began to twitter and sing among the branches, while now and
then a lark rose on the wing, and I could also hear the peculiar notes of the
robin, which bird I have never before seen in Japan.

With the exception of the twittering of the birds, the silence of the
place was unbroken; but once we were startled by a chorus of yells, which
came from a lot of ragged grass-cutters, who live a wild kind of life up
here, dwelling in buts, and carrying hay down to the neighboring villages.
Soon after we heard the loud report of a gun, as these fellows sometimes

shoot as well as mow; and the Japanese tell great stories about the deer, foxes, wolves, bears, and other animals to be met with in the woods.

At last, we arrived at the place where the regular ascent of the mountain begins, and beyond which the horses could not go. So we sent the horses and coolies away, and prepared for the hard climb before us. We had antic-ipated finding a place suitable for taking a substantial breakfast to start upon. But in this we were disappointed; for though there was a dilapi-dated shanty, not a person was to be found, and there was nothing to be seen save desolation and disorder. After considerable difficulty we man-aged to light a fire, and into it I threw a can of mutton and peas, for lack of any thing to cook them in. The two Japanese ate balls of rice, which they happened to have in their pockets, or rather, sleeves, while I waited for the mutton and peas to get heated. But our cooking arrangements did not succeed, so we ate things half-raw; and after this scanty breakfast started on our way, light in stomach, if not in heart.

The route now lay through dense woods, and the path was very narrow, being a mere gully, with an abundance of rocks and roots to hinder the way. In every respect it was far inferior to the smooth path to be found on the other side of the mountain; here and there huge trees lay across the way, completely blocking it, and broken branches and uptorn roots were scattered about, as the results of previous storms. The woods became less inviting as we proceeded, and many of the trees were old and rotten, look-ing as though they could easily topple over on us. There was a great vari-ety to be met with, and the Jap student was greatly surprised at seeing trees he had never heard of before. The birch-trees looked very curious to him; they were unusually large, and their white trunks rose up like mighty pil-lars on all sides. The maple was abundant, and the oak and various species of pine skirted the mountain for a long distance.

All the way up the mountain there are little huts or shanties, placed at intervals of half a mile or more, and during the pilgrim season these shanties are open and occupied by mountain-keepers, who make a consid-erable number of pennies by furnishing pilgrims with water and rice during the day, and a hard floor or mat to sleep upon at night. Glad would we have been to have had even such humble accommodations available to us; but as we passed one station after another we found the occupants gone, and every trace of them cleared out for the winter, so that not even a cup of water could we get for our thirsty lips. It seems the season usually closes about the 6th of September, and that the mountain-keepers had come down only the day before we went up. Consequently, we found ourselves alone on the mountain, and we scarcely knew whether there was a single person within ten miles of us.

This was not very assuring, especially as we had nothing left to eat, except a small piece of bread and a little sugar. We kept on though, and as we reached the fifth shanty we crossed a ridge, which gave us an excellent view over the treetops; with the aid of the glass we could see an immense distance, the line of sea-coast stretching out before us like a chart. We also took a somewhat disheartened look towards the top of old Fuji, which now appeared almost in a perpendicular line over our heads. Something lively was evidently going on up there, for the clouds were sweeping wildly over the summit, as if to shroud it from all intrusion.

On leaving this station the real climbing fairly commenced, and for *five hours* we worked our way up that terrible steep. The pine-trees became very, small and thinly scattered as we amended, until at last there was nothing left but a low, shrub-like growth of fir. These stunted little trees, or bushes, were very curious, being scarcely a foot high, and showing in every tough, outspreading branch the effects of trying to grow in the region of hurricanes. Beyond the line of vegetation there is absolutely nothing but black, coke-like masses of lava and reddish scoriæ and loose fragments of stone, which roll and slip under your feet as you proceed, making it extremely difficult to walk.

Before emerging from the woods we were surprised at meeting a man coming down the mountain, for we supposed nobody to be nearer us than the people of the village we had passed early in the morning. But this man reported that a party of half a dozen pilgrims were in a hut a mile or so from the summit, waiting their chance to venture to the top. They had been there for two or three days, and were entirely out of food, and this man was on his way to the village to bring them rice. There were also two or three other persons at a place not so far up, where a shrine was situated dedicated to the god of the mountain. In front of the idols, here was an immense pile of old straw shoes, thrown there by hundreds of pilgrims who had been there years before. One old man was purposely fasting up here, and had a vow not to speak for a certain time, thinking thereby to gain the favor of the gods. As we kept on up the ascent, we heard the mournful sound of a deep-toned horn echoing through the woods; the guide said it was blown in supplication to the deities to remove the storm from the mountaintop, so that the pilgrims might go up and worship.

Finally, we came to a low stone hut, where the half-dozen pilgrims were huddled together, waiting an opportunity to go to the summit. We managed to secure a little rice here, which we devoured eagerly; then I told my two companions to come along up the mountain. But the men had thoroughly frightened them out of the idea of venturing to the top, and they tried hard to back out. The roaring of the wind could be distinctly heard in the hut as it swept over the summit, and they said it was certain destruction to go up there; and that the stones were flying through the air by the force of the storm. The two Japs said they were already half dead, and for some time it was hard for me to overcome either their fatigue or fright, and induce them to resume the rocky ascent, which now became steeper at every step. At last, we got a mile farther up, and had only three more stone huts to pass ere reaching the top. It was necessary to rest repeatedly, for one's strength failed every few rods.

The path could no longer be traced, and we had to clamber on hands and knees over the shapeless masses of black lava, and were well bruised if we happened to slip. It was hard to keep up sufficient courage to advance at all, but having fairly set out, not only was I determined to reach the top, but I was also anxious to obtain accurate measurement of the height of the mountain. For this purpose, I had brought the proper instruments, which were in my Swiss knapsack, carried by the guide. I thought, if possible, I would gain the edge of the crater, then make the observations with the instruments, and hurry down again. So, pushing on in advance of the others, I waited now and then till they came in sight (for the gathering clouds hid us continually from each other), and then I would hurry on again.

Finally, I passed the last stone hut, and waited a few hundred feet above it, on a ridge of black boulders, till my companions reached the hut. I placed a small American flag (which had once waved in Sunday-school processions at home) upon the end of my long staff, and signaled my companions to come up where I stood. But they made great shouts, and beckoned me to come down; I could not hear what they said, but supposed they would soon follow, so I passed out of sight over the ridge, and with great difficulty clambered towards the edge of the crater. The wind was now so furious, and I was so utterly exhausted, that I could not keep my feet, and was again and again blown over by the severe gusts. I had to nestle behind the big boulders, or in the crevices of the lava, to keep from being tumbled over the steep places. I managed to gain a comparatively sheltered place, in a gully near the crater, and here I sat down by a snow-bank, and ate snow, waiting for the guide to come up with the knapsack containing my instruments. The wind was still furious, and fragments of stone, with showers of scoriæ, whistled by my head, causing me to dodge behind a boulder at every fresh gust and fusillade. After waiting half an hour, I crawled over to the crumbled and broken edge of the crater, where the lava evidently had once poured itself out in a vast torrent down the steep declivity. A broad, deep gully marked its course, and the broken and jagged lips of the crater bore many traces of the severe convulsions, which formerly had taken place there.

Not wishing to be blown over the edge, I made a careful retreat, and reached the snow-bank in safety. The temptation to eat snow was very great, as I could not stop my thirst; putting some in a handkerchief, I carried it down towards my companions. On approaching the stone hut where they were last seen, I was unable to attract their attention; but supposing they were asleep, I searched all about the hut. They were nowhere to be found, and the suspicion came over my mind that they had deserted me, and retreated down the mountain. I hardly knew what to do, for a storm was gathering below me, and the clouds were drifting up the slope into my face; there was no place of shelter, for even the little huts were blocked up securely with stones at their entrance, not to be opened till after the winter.

Cold and exhausted as I was, with the guide running away, and no visible path to follow, and darkness not far off, the prospect was not very cheerful; but what discomfited me more than all was the idea of having my instruments carried down the mountain, thus rendering all my plans of measuring the height futile, just at the moment when I had really gained the top!

After a great deal of severe tumbling I came in sight of the runaways, and made them halt; I restrained the lively inclination to roll them over the nearest precipice, and contented myself with scolding one in English and the other in Japanese. They made a multitude of excuses, but confessed they would have gone all the way down if they could. One said he spit so much blood that he was afraid to go higher, and the other said he could not give his life for my instruments. He was so faint for want of food, and so exhausted from the hardships he had endured, that he had fallen many times from weakness, and showed his blue and swollen limbs in proof of what he said. A friend of one of them had been lost the year before on the mountain, by being swept off by the wind. This, combined with the stories of other victims told them by the pilgrims below, frightened them from the attempt at getting any nearer the top.

It was now too late to reach the summit again, even if we had strength to do so; I therefore took tile instruments and tried to content myself with measuring the height where I was. But we were now far down the mountain, and the barometer stood a little above 20.50 inches, which would give about 11,000 feet; the thermometer was fifty-five degrees in the shade (but it was very much colder than this at the top). I estimated the distance

I had descended from the crater, and came to the conclusion that Fuji-Yama measured a little more than 11,560 feet in height. Subsequent observations, made with greater care, have proved that I was nearly right.

We hurried down the mountain, through the storm of rain, which now poured up against us, until we arrived at Station No. 5. Here we tried to obtain something to eat, but did not succeed; so we broke the only piece of bread we had into three pieces, and after eating it continued down the mountain. Darkness was now coming on rapidly, and it was hastened by the heavy clouds, which shut in upon us, and by the endless waste of woods through which we had to pass. The path was broken and rocky, and entangled with so many roots that it was very hard to traverse after all we had been through. But night was already upon us, and our lantern the guide had left at the station where we had sent away the horses in the morning; so we must push on, and that quickly, otherwise we would soon be hopelessly shut in for the night in that miserable forest, without shelter or covering. How we managed to get through I hardly know, for it was in total darkness and a drenching rain that we emerged at last from the woods and found our lantern, which was only a paper one. It was still six miles to the nearest village, and not a solitary house would we meet on the way; so as I stretched myself on the floor of the hut, I felt inclined to stay there for the night. But one of the Japs was so afraid of the wolves (!) which frequented the neighborhood, that he would not listen to the proposal; besides, we could have no fire, no light, no food, and no covering, and even if we got through the night, we would find ourselves too stiff and faint in the morning to walk. There was no alternative, therefore, but to resume the journey; so, we staggered along through the mud and clay, slipping and falling, and losing our light every few minutes by the wind and rain beating into our paper lantern. A weary time we had of it, but at last, we arrived at the village, and were hospitably received at the temple. After a hot bath and a scanty supper, I found myself stretched on the floor in a spacious room, with nothing to disturb me but the rats, and soon I was fast asleep.

We arrived here about eleven o'clock P.M.; and as we had started out on the day's undertaking at precisely two o'clock in the morning, we had endured twenty-one hours of almost uninterrupted fatigue.

In returning from Fuji-Yama we passed through the rolling section of country described my visit to the White-Rope Waterfall, where comical experiences and primitive bathtubs awaited us at the old-fashioned farmhouse.

In the lower levels of the country, and on the sunny hill-slopes facing to the south, we found the large tea districts for which this province is noted. A very large proportion of the tea exerted from Japan to the United States comes from this Province of Suruga, in which I lived. I was therefore much interested in watching the cultivation of the tea-plant, and visited the fields frequently to see the leaf prepared.

The tea-bushes are not more than breast-high full growth, and the young plants are quite small When first set out they are allowed to grow three years before any of the leaves are taken; after that the leaves are freshly picked each season, yet the plant thrives, and lives about a man's lifetime.

The plant is never stripped entirely, but only the bright green leaves are plucked which appear on top of the bush in the spring and summer. If the older leaves are ever picked, it is simply to make a coarser and cheaper quality of tea. The very finest quality, and that which costs several dollars a pound, even in the province where it is produced, is made entirely of the delicate shoots found at the tip end of the stem, in early spring, just as the tiny leaf is in process of forming. These minute shoots are carefully picked first, and the leaves below them are gathered afterwards.

Upon approaching the tea-fields, we find numbers of young girls and women scattered among the bushes, and busily engaged in filling their baskets with the fresh leaves. They are chatting merrily together, and to our Yankee eyes it seems like a good-sized huckleberrying party in New England; for the style of picking is the same and the bushes are similar, only instead of yielding berries they bear nothing but leaves. The women, young and old 'keep their tongues going as briskly during the tea-picking as their sisters of other climes are accustomed to do at their tea-drinking socials; so that the little leaf begins and ends in gossip.

When the baskets are full, they are taken to a long low house where several men are silently at work. Here they are boiled about three minutes to tender, and after being pressed between mats and dried a little, they are placed in small quantities upon a series of stout pasteboard trays or pans, set upon brick ovens containing smoldering embers of charcoal and straw.

These queer-looking pans are ranged in rows, and are maintained at various temperatures, some being so hot that you can barely put your hand on them. In front of each pan stands a Japanese, working and rolling the leaves between his hands and spreading them back and forth, to keep them equally heated throughout. The men are fine-looking fellows, but are naked as they were born, except the little sash around their loins, to which their pipe-cases and tobacco-boxes are attached.

It is here that the hard work of the tea-making process is seen. These men stand from morning until night over these slow fires, rubbing and rolling the leaves between their hands continually. The leaves are placed on the hottest pans first, when they are moist and green; but after being rolled and partially dried, they are allowed to coot on straw mats, and then they are placed on a second pan, and rubbed and rolled again. This process is repeated twenty times or more, and is far more laborious than any one would suppose.

Gradually the leaves become drier and darker in color, and after the last rolling, they are spread on moderately warm pans, and then placed in large baskets. On an average one man will roll and dry, in a whole day, as many leaves as would fill an ordinary tea-chest.

The next process consists in sifting and sorting the leaves; this is done in another house, where young girls are seated around low tables with piles of tea in front of them. Before sorting the tea, it is well shaken in sieves of various sizes, to rid it of dust and fine particles; then it is heaped upon the tables. Each girl takes her left hand full of the leaves, and throws them before her on the table, while with her right hand she picks out any stray stick, straw, or imperfect leaf, and then sweeps the rest to one side. This is done with great rapidity, and their fingers move in the same way as a hen uses her beak in pecking at corn.

The tea is sometimes still further sorted, when it is desirable to separate the fine, small leaves from the larger ones; the former always constitute the best qualities of tea, while the latter form the chief bulk of that exported to foreign countries. Of course, the best tea remains in Japan and the poorest goes abroad; but as foreigners usually spoil the true flavor with milk and sugar, it does not make so much difference after all.

The exported tea has to be "re-fired" at Yokohama. This is done on an immense scale in large stone houses, where hundreds of men and women are employed in heating and stirring the leaves again, and putting a finishing touch on the whole process; this is absolutely essential to preserve the tea and render it fit for transportation. The fresh tea odors which greet one in passing the open windows of these tea-firing establishments would make some of our old lady friends smack their lips with delight. These were the pleasant odors that I noticed on first landing at Yokohama, and which were mentioned in the first chapter.

Chapter 7

Removal to Tokyo

The long exile in Shidz-u-o-ka was drawing to a close. The Government had determined to centralize the educational interests at the capital, and the provincial schools were suffered temporarily to decline. The old feudal system was abolished; the Mikado had transferred his court to Tokyo, which heretofore had been the capital of the military chief, or Tycoon. The latter had retired with his retainers to Shidz-u-o-ka, which became the St. Helena of Tycoonism. The men who formerly ruled Japan were therefore my associates and advisers in Shidz-u-o-ka. But their successors at the Mikado's capital found themselves unable to manage the affairs of government, hitherto left in the hands of the Tycoon. They had not the practical skill to guide the ship of state with steadiness through the troubled waters of political change.

Therefore, they sent to Shidz-u-o-ka and called away my friends and my brightest students, assigning them important positions at the capital. Against this course, I protested in a memorial to the " Mom-bu-sho, " or Department of Education. The officials replied that Shidz-u-o-ka should feet complimented in being called upon to furnish young men for important positions in the capital. This was cold comfort, and I urged that the best students should be allowed to remain until the completion of their course. I also argued that no education was truly national which disregarded the interests of the interior.

The Educational Department admitted the truthfulness of the argument, of which they have since experienced the demonstration; yet my protests were unavailing, and the Government continued to call away my most valued friends and helpers. Katz and Okubo, who had been instrumental in bringing me to Japan, and had always been my best advisers, were called to the capital; the former resumed his old position as Admiral of the Navy, and the latter became Governor of Tokyo. Nakamura, Shimojo, and all of my foremost students removed to the capital, saying that every thing was now changing in Japan, and that I should soon be called away also.

New governors were appointed over the province, who knew not Joseph," and my old friends faded out, leaving me alone. My enthusiasm was dampened in seeing my cherished plans thwarted, and the labor of building up any permanent work appeared in vain.

I lived alone in the new house during the second year, and the sense of solitude became very oppressive. No one lived near me except the servants, who occupied the little Japanese building near the gate. At night, I sat in my room listening to the wind sighing through the pines that skirted the embankment of the moat. The screech of the night owl could be heard, and the timid bark of the foxes who frequented the ruins of the castle. Now and then an earthquake would startle my reveries, sending meat a

rapid pace out upon the balcony, where I had an outdoor view of the phe-
nomena. The ground shook and heaved, the moat trembled, the treetops
swayed, the heavy house creaked and groaned, and the windows rattled as
though they would break. The birds, frightened from their perches on the
treetops, flew wildly around, uttering piteous cries; the mountains looked
as though they were ready to "skip like rams, and the little hills like
lambs." But the stars twinkled silently, as though they never could shake,
and soon all became quiet again.

During the long winter evenings, the stars were my best companions; I
never wearied of studying them through my little telescope, and they were
always found bright and cheerful. The country people on the mountains
near Shidz-u-o-ka sometimes set fire to the long dry grass of that desolate
region at night. The whole mountain chain appeared at times in flames,
and a fiery circle swept around the "peaceful hills," as the name Shidz-u-o-
ka signifies. One could easily imagine that half a dozen volcanoes had broken out, and the first time I witnessed the startling scene I thought
Fuji-Yama's volcanic fires were starting afresh, and that perhaps Shidz-u-
o-ka would become another Pompeii. In the daytime, the mountains
looked blackened and bare, as though they had gone into deep mourning.

At the close of the second year at Shidz-u-o-ka an official order came,
calling me to the Imperial College in Tokyo.[32] I did not accept the new
appointment very promptly, even though my loneliness and exile would
be at an end, for I should have American and English society there.
Finally, I submitted certain conditions to the Department of Education,
which were accepted; whereupon I prepared to remove to the capital.

The three conditions were afterwards fulfilled satisfactorily. The first
condition was, that I should have the chair of chemistry only assigned to
me at the Tokyo College; secondly, that my philosophical apparatus

---

[32] Now Tokyo University.

should go with me; and thirdly, that a good house should be assigned me in place of the one I left at Shidz-u-o-ka.

Moving in Japan is not very easy work; but at last, all my furniture was packed, and sent off to a seaport six miles distant, to be shipped on a Japanese junk. Every thing was done up in straw, making huge bundles and bales of every possible description. A long train of carts left the house one morning, loaded with my household effects. Each cart had a naked Jap pulling like a horse in front, while a woman pushed the cart behind, and children tugged at the wooden wheels, or pulled ahead with short ropes. The procession of carts made the most ridiculous freight-train I ever beheld; yet these poor people drew the cumbersome loads all the way to the seaport, for human labor is cheaper than that of horses, and each cart only cost half a dollar.

Six huge boxes containing philosophical apparatus, which could not be sent by sea, were subsequently carried on men's shoulders all the way to Tokyo, over the Hakoné Mountains, a distance of one hundred miles!

The junk was obliged to pass around Cape Idzu, a bold promontory, which may be seen in the map. This cape is the dread of all the sailors of the region, and many a junk each year finds its tragic end among the rocky boulders and surging waves which encompass the cape. The French steamer Nil was lost here; and one of Commodore Perry's steamers once grounded on the treacherous coast.

If even foreign ships were thus endangered, I had little hope for the safety of my dilapidated junk during a stormy winter voyage. The junk was only fifty feet long, and the goods were stowed away under a bamboo roof, in the middle of the boat; the salt spray dashed over the junk, freezing the straw mats into icy-coverings, while the boatmen shivered around a small fire kept burning in the hold.

Months passed without my hearing any thing of the junk, and I finally gave it up for lost, and bade farewell to my earthly possessions; but at last it appeared, one frosty morning, among the crowded and forlorn-looking craft of Tokyo, covered with ice and saturated with salt. I was delighted to see it, however, in any shape; for it not only had my furniture and library on board, but hundreds of beautiful presents given in years past by the Japanese, which I should have been very sorry to lose. My journey to Tokyo was rapidly made, compared with the time first required in going over the same ground, when the yaconims met me at every town and village. The Tokaido had become an old story to me, for I had made the distance to Yokohama many times since my first journey, and every place on the long road was now familiar.

Once I took a flying trip to Yokohama in company with a jumping toothache, which quickened my progress considerably, so that the journey was made in a day and a half. But then I had the ex-Tycoon's horse and carriage, and rode to the foot of the Hakoné Pass. However, the poor horse gave up the ghost the next day, for Japanese horses cannot endure as much as the jinrikisha men, especially when the driver has a toothache!

After painful chloroform experiences in Yokohama, I returned to Shidz-u-o-ka on a steam-yacht, formally presented by Queen Victoria to the Tycoon; the United States consul was on board the yacht, together with a party of naval officers from the United States flag-ship Colorado. They paid me a very pleasant visit at my temple-home, where I entertained them as well as I could, though half of them had to sleep on the floor; afterwards they went off on a trip through the tea district. During their stay at Shidz-u-o- ka, their bright uniforms greatly astonished the country people. They returned by the steam-yacht to Yokohama.

I made many trips on the Tokaido, and excursions into the neighboring provinces, of which there is not space for me to speak. But I cannot forbear mentioning the romantic feelings with which I finally returned to Yokohama, after being shut up so long in the interior of Japan. When I first landed in the country, and journeyed into the lonely isolation that awaited me so far away from friends, it appeared a strange dream, conducting my senses outside the world and all its familiar associations. But when I turned back again, leaving the pagan surroundings in which I had at last become so much at home, and re-entered the business life and social atmosphere of a civilized and Christian community, it seemed a greater dream than the other! Yokohama is to all intents a foreign city set down upon Japanese soil, and although it may look queer and quaint enough to all new-comers, from whatever land they hail, yet a Jap fresh from the provinces of the interior sees more to astonish his awestruck eyes than a verdant Vermont youth would experience in his first visit to New York City. The regular and paved streets, the substantial stone houses, the elegant shop windows, the fine equipages, the foreign style of dress, and the busy life of the people, all combine to produce an effect upon the bewildered senses of the country Jap, the like of which he never knew before.

And when he strolls along the water-quay and looks out towards those leviathan steamers which lie at anchor in the bay, or when, perhaps, he goes to the railroad depot and timidly asks for his ticket for the next train to Tokyo, it begins to dawn on his mind that the nineteenth century is finding its way into his long-secluded country, and that the outside barbarians are not such offensive creatures after all.

On entering Yokohama after my long residence apart from foreign society, I looked upon the city with something of the wonder and curiosity of a veritable Japanese; and the first thing I proposed to my companions from Shidz-u-o-ka was a ride on the railroad just completed between Yokohama and Tokyo.

We saw the locomotive and train coming as we turned down the hill towards the city, and the naked Japs who pulled our jinrikishas looked in astonishment at the smoking locomotive, wondering what kind of an animal it could be! In journeying along the Tokaido, the newly constructed telegraph followed us the whole way from Shidz-u-o-ka, and the little wire seemed like a thread that bound me to civilization. The country people have a great deal of superstition about it, and dislike to have the wire cross their rice-fields; for they say the evil spirits prevent the crops from growing. At first, the ignorant farmers used to cut the wire, and throw stones at the glass insulators on the poles; they would also watch the wire for hours to see the messages go by! What the crazy foreigners had stretched the wire across the country for, they could not imagine; but at last, they ceased to trouble their heads about it, and left the telegraph alone. But the railroad was far more wonderful; of *that* they could see the meaning, though the locomotive was entirely beyond their comprehension.

The road is only eighteen miles long, and there is a substantial stone depot at each terminus. The Yokohama station is very handsome, and all the arrangements are complete. When I took my first ride on the railroad I was accompanied by a little boy who formerly lived with me, and who was now going to his father, the new Governor of Tokyo. The little fellow had never heard of a railroad train, and when we were fairly seated in the car, he looked around, wondering what kind of a little house we were in, with its curious doors and sliding windows. When the train began moving slowly out of the depot he grasped the seat with a look of terror, and glanced anxiously into my face to see if I was frightened also. But finding that I only laughed at his fears, he regained courage enough to look out of the window at the trees and houses, which began to fly by us faster and faster. The first time the car stopped he ran out on the platform and peered under the wheels to see what was pushing it along; but when we passed one of the down trains he looked at the locomotive, and seemed at last to realize that this was the big black horse that was doing it all. In half an hour, we arrived at Shin-a-ga-wa, a distance which it used to take more than half a day to journey over, and which brought us to the suburbs of Tokyo. Here we took jinrikishas, with naked Japs, to draw us two miles more into the heart of the city.

On arriving at the capital, I reported myself at the Mombusho Department, where I had an interview with the Minister of Education. He received me very kindly, and stated that Mr. Hatakéyama, the newly appointed Director of the Imperial College, would confer with me there respecting my new duties in the institution.

Now it so happened that Hatakéyama was my warmest Japanese friend, whom I had known for several years in America, but who had changed his name on returning to his country, so that I did not at first recognize him.

In the United States, his name was Soo-gi-woo-ra; but this was an assumed title, and now he had resumed his family name.

He was one of the first students who left Japan to study in foreign countries, shortly after the bombardment of his native city, Kag-o-shi-ma, by the English war-ships. After remaining a year in England, he came to the United States, and eventually settled down to his studies at New Brunswick, N. J., where I first met him at Rutgers College. He was quite a lad when he left his native land, and his mother was very anxious about him, for she had heard strange stories about the barbarians who were reported as living in England and America. With a mother's solicitude she urged him to take a few bags of good wholesome rice with him, for she had been told that people in America lived on snakes, frogs, and lizards!

He became a Christian at New Brunswick, and joined the Second Reformed Church. When called to an account for this act by the government, he replied that he had come abroad to study into the true source of western civilization, and he found Christianity to be that source, therefore he had embraced it. The power of Christian countries did not consist in cannonballs and gunpowder, as he had been led to believe when his native city was bombarded by the English; but there was a better principle underlying civilization, which had peace and love and religious life as its basis. His reason endorsed Christianity, and his whole heart accepted it.

Instead of the government calling him back to his own country and punishing him, as he had cause to fear- for Christianity was forbidden in Japan, and at one time was punishable with death - they placed more confidence in him than ever, and gave him the superintendence of the other students who were subsequently sent to pursue their studies in America.

At New Brunswick, he was very earnest in his desire that I should go and help the cause of civilization in Japan, and before I started for that country, he came up to see me in Albany. After spending a pleasant evening with some friends, we went to the depot near the Hudson River Bridge, and bade each other *Sayoonara* - good-bye; and as the train moved off, Hatakéyama said, "You go westward while I go eastward, and we will meet around the world in Japan!"

I started from the same depot across the continent, and passed over the broad Pacific, while he sailed over the Atlantic; but owing to his joining the Japanese Embassy, with which he traveled through all the countries and courts of Europe, he did not reach Japan until two years later, at the time I was called from Shidz-u-o-ka to Tokyo. My surprise and pleasure may therefore be imagined when the Minister of Education informed me that Hatakéyama was now the new director of the college, and that he would consult with me concerning the duties and details, which heretofore were contested with yaconims and petty officials.

Accordingly, I went gladly to the reception- room of the Kai-sei Gak-ko,[33] or college building, and awaited the coming of him who was at once my old friend and my new yaconim! The officials sat around in dignified silence, when the door opened and the new Director stepped in. He was greeted by my attendants and others with profound bows; and as I approached unobserved behind, and spoke his familiar name, he turned about with the same joyous bound as of yore, grasping my hands with the grip of bygone days, and burst forth with such a gleeful warmth of welcome as made the solemn officials look at one another with mingled awe and wonder, that such a boisterous breach of etiquette should come from one who usually was so dignified and calm. We cared little what they thought, however, and enjoyed ourselves for some time as hilariously as we pleased.

Hatakéyama said he had "piles of things" to tell me about his strange experiences in the various courts of Europe, and he afterwards gave me the most vivid descriptions of all that he had seen and heard. His official connection with the embassy afforded him rare opportunities of meeting many of the greatest men and princes in Europe. He did not forget to bring me some pictures he had promised from my old home in Geneva,

---

[33] Tokyo University (Tokyo Imperial University until 1945)

Switzerland; and I also gave him some large photographs of Niagara, which he requested me to bring from the falls for his mother.

The new Director assigned me my duties and residence at the college, and I was soon settled amid the novel experiences of life at the capital. I took new courage, and began my labors afresh.

Shortly after, the Saga rebellion broke out in the southern provinces of Japan, and Hatakéyama was sent down there in company with the former prince of his province to try and conciliate the insurgents. The attempt was unsuccessful, and a short but bloody strife ensued, in which many noble lives were lost; among others, my former student and friend Katski, who studied with me in Albany, was beheaded with eleven of the leaders of the rebellion. Katski was a fine young fellow, and his cruel death was a great shock to me; I had endeavored to persuade him not to go back to his province, when the rebellion first broke out, but he would not heed the advice.

When Hatakéyama started for Saga I expressed some apprehensions respecting his safety. He only smiled, and said quietly, " My trust is in the Lord, and my true faith will sustain me." I had a long interview with him at his house before he left for the south, concerning the re- establishment of my Bible-classes in Tokyo, especially at the Imperial College. He expressed surprise that no Bible-classes had been established there before, but said that as the law against Christianity had not been revoked, he was not officially able to give the permission desired. Personally, however, he said that he wished the plan God-speed, and as Director, he would appear blind to any attempt that I might see fit to make. He wished most heartily, he said, that the young men of Japan might study the Gospel and abide by it.

Accordingly, I started three Bible-classes in Tokyo. Two were held in my house near the college, and one at the house of my friend Nakamura, where my old friends and students from Shidz - u - o - ka were gathered together. The students of the college were only permitted to leave the grounds on Sunday, which had hitherto been simply their holiday; although I needed the Sabbath for rest, after the week's hard work, I appointed the Bible-class for students from the scientific department at eight o'clock in the morning, and the class for students from the legal department at seven in the evening.

The other Bible-class was held at Nakamura's, two miles from the college, at three o'clock in the afternoon. Here I was warmly welcomed by my Shidz-u-o-ka friends who had removed to Tokyo, and I continued the class for many months, finally giving it over to a missionary from Canada, for whom Nakamura built a house.

Nakamura had a piece of ground at the top of a hill called "Christian Slope," where he said lie wished to have a church built before very long. It will be remem-bered that he once petitioned the government to build a Christian church, so as to give the new religion a fair trial! This "Christian Slope," near his house, was so called from a Jesuit missionary who was confined there in prison more than two centuries ago, for attempting to teach Christianity. The government would not permit the people to go near him, but still he succeeded in converting his jailer.

Soon after arriving in Tokyo I attended a New Year's reception held at the educational department, at which all the foreign professors of the Imperial College were present. The body of instructors assembled were the most cultured and gentlemanly company I had met in Japan, and it was a pleasure to see the progressive interests of the country entrusted to such competent hands.

The new building of the Kaisei Gakko, or Imperial College, was opened with imposing ceremonies by the Mikado shortly before I came to Tokyo. It was decorated with flags of every nationality, and presented a beautiful appearance. The building covers several acres, and has three long wings extending 192 feet to the rear. Behind these are the gymnasium, dining-hall, and storehouses. The first floor of the main building contains the library, laboratories, and lecture- rooms. The English department occupied the central wing, and the French and German departments the right and left wings. The second story throughout the building was used as a dormitory, for most of the students lived here.

In front of the main entrance was a grassy mound and high gateway; the latter is shown wide open in the picture. In passing this gate, every student was obliged to leave a wooden ticket marked with his name. This was returned to him when he came back to the college. The rules and regulations governing the students were very strict.

In the picture of the gateway, the name "Kaisei Gakko" is seen on the right pillar, in Chinese characters; my friend Dr. Veeder, the professor of physics, is standing in the center of the picture with a few of his students around him; some of them are in regulation dress, and others in native costume. The other view which is given of the Kaisei Gakko presents the front of the building as it appeared the day that the Mikado visited and opened the institution.

Chapter 8

Rambles About the Capital

Life in Tokyo was more varied than that at Shidz-u-o-ka. Something was always going on, and pleasant society was not wanting, whenever one felt the need of it. Evening parties and entertainments were frequent among the foreign residents, and the elegance and style seen on such occasions reminded one more of fashionable life at home than of residence in a pagan city.

The capital itself is not beautiful. There are no elegant boulevards or splendid buildings, such as those seen in European countries. Toque is simply a vast wilderness of houses, containing nearly a million souls, but lacking all the evidences of comfort and luxury to be found in the capitals of western lands. The houses are built of wood, and a general view of the city presents an endless succession of tiled and shingled roofs, with here and there a fireproof storehouse, having walls of white cement. Yet, there are places of great interest to visit, notwithstanding the sameness and shabbiness of the city. Let us stand for a moment on the highest wall of the Tokyo castle, built by the same great chieftain who constructed the castle at Shidz-u- o-ka. Close beside us is a large cannon, which is fired every day precisely at noon. All about us are the deep moats, massive walls, and colossal gateways of the castle, encircling a space of nearly a mile in extent, and forming a wilderness of walls, embankments, public buildings, and shady promenades, right in the heart of the city. At each angle of the castle wall there used to be a square tower, built of stone and covered with white cement; the tower had narrow windows, from which arrows could be discharged, and the roof was made of heavy stone tiles, stamped with the crest of the Tycoon. Only a few of these towers now remain, the rest having been removed by order of the Mikado's government.

The picture represents a portion of the castle moat and wall, where the three-storied towers are still standing. The moat is filled with water.

There are also numerous canals, which intersect the city in every direction, so that merchandise can be transported from one point to another. Boats of every description are poled or sculled through the canals. I had a little canoe carrying but one person, and propelled swiftly by a single paddle. In this canoe, I cruised around the canals and moats of the capital, studying many phases of life among the boatmen and fishermen, which could not otherwise be observed. Frequently I would venture out upon the bay, but the canoe (which I called " The Rob Roy of Tokyo," and which only drew two inches of water) would dance on the waves like a duck, while the salt spray washed over the thin deck, threatening to upset me. But it never did.

Sometimes I drew in my spoon-like paddle and raised an umbrella to the wind. The canoe would scud across the bay, greatly to the astonishment of the Japanese fishermen, who had never seen such a tiny craft before.

A large river emptied into the Bay of Yedo on the eastern side of the city, which may be seen in the small map of Tokyo and vicinity. Near the mouth of the river was the small "concession," where foreign merchants and missionaries resided. Here were the foreign consulates, stores, schools, and chapels. Foreigners in the service of the Japanese Government alone were allowed to reside outside the limits of the "concession" at the capital; for Japan was not yet free to foreign trade, excepting five open ports.

The most beautiful and interesting places in Tokyo, and those, which I most frequently visited, were the large temples of Shiba, Uyéno, and Asakusa. The two former were the burial-places of the Tycoons for several centuries, and their sacred groves, richly ornamented shrines, and spacious halls for worship were the most beautiful works of art of ancient Japan. Both temples are situated in the suburbs of Tokyo, on opposite sides of the city, and their broad avenues and overarching trees afford splendid promenades for the people. The temple grounds serve the purpose of parks. At Uyéno, the large buildings were burned during a battle fought there in 1868, between the forces of the Mikado and the retainers of the Tycoon. The gateway leading to the grounds is still riddled with musket balls, and the trees are scarred by bullets. Only the tombs and a few smaller temples remain.

But at Shiba, the temples are well preserved, and the carvings and gildings are very elegant. The eaves, pillars, and portals of the temples display figures of every possible variety, from the hideous scales and claws of the frightful dragon to the soft white plumage of the sacred crane. Massive bronze lanterns, six feet high, are ranged in rows in the courtyard, and covered corridors lead up the hillside to the tombs of the Tycoons.

There are six of these tombs, similar to the one built for the first Tycoon at the Temple of Kuno, near Shidz-u-o-ka. The picture gives an excellent idea of this tomb, with the Tycoon's crest upon it.

The tomb consists of a hollow cylinder of stone, placed upon a granite pedestal, and surmounted by an immense capstone weighing several tons. The dead body of the Tycoon is deposited in the tomb in a square casket, or sometimes in a large earthen jar; for the Japanese are buried in a sitting posture, and occupy but little space. The tomb is closed by a bronze door, upon which a large crest of the Tycoon is seen. This crest resembles three outspread cloverleaves, turned inward upon each other. It is found stamped upon every thing throughout the temple grounds, even upon the stone tiles of the massive temple roofs.

Although the first Tycoon was buried nearly three hundred years ago at the Temple of Kuno, which he built for himself on a high cliff overlooking the sea, near Shidz-u-o-ka, yet all of his successors were buried at Tokyo. The most beautiful building at Kuno was a five-storied pagoda (like the one seen in Chapter III.), which towered above the tall cypress trees. This pagoda was taken down by order of the government, because it was characteristic of Buddhism, and they wished to make Kuno a Shinto shrine, in accordance with the ancient Japanese religion. From the ruins of the beautiful pagoda, I obtained a large golden crest of the Tycoon, which had long glistened in the sunlight across the Pacific.

When the government attempted to change the largest temple at Shiba into a Shinto shrine also, the devout Buddhists were so enraged that they set fire to the beautiful temple, and burned it to the ground. It made a magnificent bonfire; and the copper sheets on the roof, and the metal ornaments, gave a green and crimson tinge to the flames.

The Japanese in Tokyo are accustomed to large fires, however; sometimes I have seen half a mile of the city in flames at once. The people cannot put out the fire, but they tear down the wooden buildings around it, and thus stay its terrible course.

The most populous part of the city is on the eastern side of the castle area, near a bridge from which all distances in Japan are said to be reckoned. A fearful conflagration swept through this district before I arrived in the city, and destroyed five thousand houses and hundreds of provincial *Yashikis*. The streets were afterwards widened and straight-tened, and the district rebuilt in foreign style- i.e., with sidewalks, gas-lamps, and two-story houses, half foreign and half Japanese. The main street was called the To-ri. This is the Broadway of Tokyo; it runs from the new railroad station to the old bridge of Nihon-Bashi. After crossing the bridge, houses of the Japanese style are seen again.

The street life in Tokyo may be studied by strolling up and down the Tori; and I frequently rambled through this street, to indulge my curiosity in observing the strange characteristics of the Japanese people. The native shops were ranged on both sides of the street, their fronts being thrown open so that the passer-by could see all the display of wares at once. The shop-keeper squatted upon the straw-matted floor, in the midst of his goods, toasting his fingers over a brazier of live coals, and smoking his tiny pipe, which was refilled at every third puff. If you stopped to purchase any small article, he would bow politely, and figure up the price on a little frame with rows of beads running on parallel wires, like the *abacus* used in schools. Unless you were expert in mental arithmetic, he would calculate faster with his fingers than you could with your brains. His result was always right.

Many of the streets crossing the Tori were devoted exclusively to the sale of special articles. Bamboo Street "looked as though a forest of long bamboo poles had sprung up through its entire length; and the "Dyers' Street," where deep vats and colored fabrics are exposed to the air, is filled with odors strong enough to knock a person over, even in passing. Some streets contain willow and basket ware; others exhibit long shelves of lac-quer-ware and cabinets, ornamented with every conceivable design. Another street contains folding screens, inscribed with pictures and poetry; still others have paper lanterns, wooden-shoe shops, silk establish-ments, bookstores with European maps suspended in front; and some streets are devoted to the sale of foreign goods, such as lamps, candles, kerosene, soap, toilet articles, and bottles of beer. The Japanese seem to think that beer and champagne are the characteristic marks of modern civ-ilization. Unfortunately, too many sad examples have been set them in this direction by foreigners from Christian countries.

The most interesting sights in the streets are the games and sports of the children. The Japanese believe in enjoying themselves, and the young folks are as bright and merry as the children of other climes. The girls play battledore and shuttlecock, and the boys fly kites and spin tops. The girls enjoy their game very much, and are usually dressed in their prettiest robes and bright-colored girdles; their faces are powdered with a little rice flour, their lips are tinted crimson, and their hair is done up in a most extraordinary fashion.

They play in the open street, sometimes forming a circle of half a dozen or more, and sending the flying shuttlecock from one to the other. They are very skillful, and rarely miss a stroke. The boys like a strong wind that their kites may soar high; but the girls sing a song that it may be calm, so that their shuttlecocks may go right.

The boys have wonderful kites, made of tough paper pasted on light bamboo frames, and decorated with dragons, warriors, and storm hobgoblins. Across the top of the kite is stretched a thin ribbon of whalebone, which vibrates in the wind, making a peculiar humming sound. When I first walked the streets of Tokyo I could not imagine what the strange noises meant that seemed to proceed from the sky above me; the sound at times was shrill and sharp, and then low and musical. At last, I discovered several kites in the air, and when the breeze freshened, the sounds were greatly increased.

Sometimes the boys put glue on their kite-strings, near the top, and dip the strings into pounded glass. Then they fight with their kites, which they place in proper positions, and attempt to saw each other's strings with the pounded glass. When a string is severed, a kite falls, and is claimed by the victor. The boys also have play-fights with their tops.

Sometimes I met boys running a race on long stilts; at other times, they would have wrestling matches, in which little six-year-old youngsters would toss and tumble one another to the ground. Their bodies were stout and chubby, and their rosy cheeks showed signs of health and happiness. They were always good-natured, and never allowed themselves to get angry.

On the fifth day of the fifth month, the boys have their Fourth of July, which they call the "Feast of Flags." They celebrate the day very peaceably, with games and toys. They have sets of figures, representing soldiers, heroes, and celebrated warriors; with flags, daimio processions, and tournaments. Outside of the house, a bamboo pole is erected by the gate, from the top of which a large paper fish is suspended. This fish is sometimes six feet long, and is hollow. When there is a breeze it fills with wind, and its tail and fins flap in the air as though it were trying to swim away. The fish is intended to show that there are boys in the family. It is the carp, which is found in Japanese waters, and swims against the stream, and leaps over waterfalls. The boys must therefore learn from the fish to persevere against all difficulties, and surmount every obstacle in life. When hundreds of these huge fishes are seen swimming in the breeze, it presents a very curious appearance.

The girls have their "Feast of Dolls" on the third day of the third month. During the week preceding this holiday, the shops of Tokyo are filled with dolls and richly dressed figures. This "Feast of Dolls" is a great gala-day for the girls. They bring out all their dolls and gorgeously dressed images, which are quite numerous in respectable families, having been kept from one generation to another; the images range from a few inches to a foot in height, and represent court nobles and ladies, with the Mikado and his household in full costume. They are all arranged on shelves, together with many other beautiful toys, and the girls present offerings of rice, fruit, and "sake" wine, and mimic all the routine of court life. The shops display large numbers of these images at this special season; after the holidays, they suddenly disappear.

I once bought a large doll baby at one of the shops, to send home to my little sister; the doll was dressed in the ordinary way, having its head shaved in the style of most Japanese babies. It was so life-like that when propped up on a chair a person would easily suppose it to be a live baby.

In going along the Tori I would often see a group of children gathered around a street storyteller, listening with widening eyes and breathless attention to the ghost story or startling romance which he was narrating. Many old folks also gathered around, and the storyteller shouted and stamped on his elevated platform, attracting great attention, until, just as the most thrilling part of the story was reached, he suddenly stopped and took up a collection! He refused to go on unless the number of pennies received was sufficient to encourage the continuation of the story.

Street theatricals can also be seen, and traveling shows with monkeys, bears, and tumbling gymnasts, who greatly amuse the children. Sugar-candy and various kinds of sweetmeats are sold by peddlers, who are eagerly sought after by the little folks. Sometimes a man carries small kitchen utensils on the ends of a pole, and serves out tiny griddlecakes to the children, who watch him cook the cakes, and smack their lips in antic-ipation of the feast. A showman will put a piece of camphor on the tiny model of a duck which be floats on a shallow dish of water, and as the chil-dren took on in wonder the dissolving camphor gum sends the duck from side to side, as though it were alive.

The boys delight in fishing, and will sit for hours holding the line by the moats and canals, waiting for a bite. I have seen a dozen people watching a single person fish, when there would not be a bite once in the half-hour.

There are few vehicles in Tokyo, excepting the jinrikishas; and most of the people walk in the middle of the street. When riding on horseback it is impossible to go at a rapid rate without endangering the youngsters who sprawl around in the street. Chickens, dogs, and cats are also in the way; the latter animal has no tail in Japan.

The greatest playground in Tokyo appears to be the garden and cluster of buildings known as the Temple of Asakusa. The temple stands near the river, at the further end of the city. Here the people congregate in large numbers for pleasure and worship; the Japanese combine religion and amusement, and their temple grounds are the places of resort on all festi-val occasions. There is a perpetual holiday at Asakusa. The man temple is approached by a long avenue, lined on both sides with booths, stalls, and shops, in which toys and all manner of things are sold. The last table is devoted to the sale of small beans, with which to feed the sacred doves that throng the eaves of the temple by hundreds. When I purchased a penny's worth of beans, threw them on the ground, the whole feathery tribe of doves descended in a fluttering cloud, and picked the beans up in an instant. At another table, larger beans are purchased to feed the sacred white horse. The horse is very gentle, and stands with due dignity in his stall, receiving with meekness all favors conferred upon him; he seems to "know beans" very well. The gods are said to ride upon this horse, therefore it is a religious act to feed him; he is plump and fat, like the lazy priest who attends him.

Inside the temple, the altars and images are protected from the birds by wire screens. There is a small wooden image, which has been rubbed by the people so that its face, hands, and feet have been literally worn off. Whosoever touches the image is said to have his diseases cured by touching the corresponding portion of his own body. It was very pitiable to see the blind, lame, and sickly coming up to this hideous wooden image, hoping to be cured thereby. To the left of the temple is a beautiful garden, with flowers, dwarfed trees, and miniature lakes. Here also is a grand display of wax figures, illustrating Japanese legends and romance; these figures are similar to those once seen at Barnum's Museum, but are more finely executed. To see these figures you pass through corridors of some length, winding through a labyrinth of passages, and coming at each turn upon new sets of groups, representing every phase of Japanese life and costume, poetical and tragical, from the farmer plodding the field to the goddess descending from the skies. At one point a fairy nymph is charming the lonely passerby with music from a stringed instrument, as she sits in a shady bower; at another place a freshly-severed head lies hideously on the floor, with eyes half closed and death pallor on the cheek, while a furious monster holds his sword aloft, as though ready to come at you as the next victim.

In the neighborhood of Asakusa is a place called Mékojima, celebrated for its cherry-blossoms. The cherry-trees line the roadside on the riverbank for a distance of two miles. They overarch the road so as to form a continuous bower, and the blossoms are so thick and flaky that the trees appear as if covered with light snow. People throng the place by thousands, and take more pleasure in their admiration of these cherry-blossoms than in any other form of amusement. Teahouses and gardens abound along the bank of the river, and mirth and music are heard on all sides. Though the trees have such beautiful blossoms, yet they bear no fruit.

My home in Tokyo was near the second moat of the great castle, in the center of the city; the house stood within a compound, or enclosure, adjoining the college buildings. Within this enclosure most of the foreign professors resided; their houses were nearly all of the same style as the one shown in the picture. The view of my house was taken in winter during a snowstorm, to show that we had at least a little snow in Tokyo. In the foreground are two jinrikishas, or little carriages such as I used in riding around Tokyo. The two little girls in one of the jinrikishas were great pets of mine; they were the daughters of a lady friend, who had charge of the Government Girls' School. Two servants are standing in the doorway, and considerable snow covers the roof. The smoke-pipe on the left of the entrance shows that the Japanese carpenter could not be prevailed upon to build a chimney. None of the houses in the compound had chimneys, and many fires have originated from the careless way in which these pipes were put up.

The photographic camera seen on the table at the left was the one employed in taking some of the pictures of this book. Near the doorstep is another table, with a sword-rack and sword presented by the Governor of Tokyo. When I first came to Tokyo I met with great pleasure my friend and former classmate, Mr. Griffis, who had once tramped with me through Switzerland, and who was now settled at the Tokyo College, after living a year at Fukwi, on the western coast of Japan. In his journey to Tokyo, he passed through Shidz-u-o-ka, when I went out to meet him with a mounted escort, and entertained him at my old temple home. At Tokyo, we lived together in the same house for several months; but after his return to America, I was left alone, as I had been at Shidz-u-o-ka. Mr. Griffis wrote a large and interesting work on Japan while living in this house, which has since been published; and if my young reader wishes a more complete history of Japan than I have space to give, I would refer him to Mr. Griffis's book, "The Mikado's Empire."

A few months after Mr. Griffis left for America I invited Hatakéyama, the Director of the Kaisei Gakko, to come and live with me. He wished to do so very much, as his own house was small and two miles away, whereas mine was large and close to the college, and very convenient. I petitioned the Minister of Education to allow Hatakéyama to change his residence, but for some unaccountable reason the request was politely declined.

The scourge of smallpox visited Tokyo while I was there; two of the professors died with it, and great alarm prevailed. The natives died by hundreds; but the Japanese seemed used to it. One of my friends at this time was suffocated from charcoal fumes in bathing in a Japanese bathtub; I helped embalm the poor fellow, so that his body might be sent home.

Quite a tragic affair occurred at the Kaisei Gakko one morning, which nearly resulted in the destruction of the whole building by fire. I was giving a lecture to my chemistry class, when suddenly great confusion was heard in the second story, and the courtyard was seen filled with smoke. Dismissing the class, and advising them to keep cool, I seized the Babcock fire extinguisher, which always stood on the table in my laboratory, and asked my two assistants to bring a pair of the same instruments which stood in the hall, and which I had newly charged the day before.

With the three Babcocks, we went upstairs, but so great was the confusion that we could not at first find the whereabouts of the fire. Beds, books, and furniture were being tumbled out of the windows, and students were rushing around like maniacs. At last, I discovered the fire in the roof of the French department. It had caught from the red-hot smoke-pipe seen projecting from the corner of the wing of the college building in the picture a little further on. The fire had smoldered for hours, and then broken out with terrible fury, sweeping along the rafters under the roof, and would soon have wrapped the whole wing in flames. A Japanese hand-pump had been brought into the room at the corner of the building; the firemen had broken a hole through the ceiling, and were waiting for water to be brought upstairs in buckets! I laughed at their clumsy machine, and mounted the ladder leading into the burning loft above. The sight that met my gaze was appalling, and startled me so that I burned and blackened my arms in trying to get through the hole with the heavy Babcock on my back. Broad sheets of flame leaped along the rafters, and the smoke was so suffocating I could scarcely breathe.

I attempted to head off the flames, knowing that if they gained much greater progress they would be beyond control, and the whole building would be sacrificed. Swinging from one rafter to another, I turned on the magic stream of the carbonic-acid-gas extinguisher, and the effect was instantaneous. Wherever the stream touched the fire it swept it out like a broom, and by the time I had emptied the first Babcock forty feet of the flames had been subdued. Meanwhile I was nearly extinguished myself by the thick smoke, and crept cautiously towards the hole, where I allowed the Jap pump to play on my face and head.

Thus revived, I took the second extinguisher, and nearly subdued the rest of the flames. As the third and last instrument was passed up to me, I heard a great noise on the roof over my head, and soon shingles and stone tiles began to fall, showing that the firemen were breaking in the roof in true Japanese fashion. In vain, I called to them to desist, and not to let in the air; and I sent a stream of acidulated water into their faces to drive them away. Still they persisted in breaking in the roof, and at the same time, men with stout poles began breaking up the thin floor beneath me. With the ingress of fresh air, the fire started up again in several places. The treacherous crossbeams were some distance apart, and it was difficult to step from one to the other with the heavy instrument on my back. One young fellow, who ventured up to help me, fell through the ceiling like a shot, and disappeared from the scene. I crouched in the corner and played on the burning rafters as best I could; reflecting on the pleasant alternative of being roasted alive, or struck on the head by a tile from above, or poked by a pole from below. A burning stick fell on my back, and warmed the situation somewhat. The extinguishers were true to their name, however, and after the third one had been emptied, the flames were so far subdued that a few buckets of water finished them.

As a touching sequel to the affair, I stayed in bed for two days afterward. This is the nearest I ever came to being cremated.

The picture presents a portion of the Kaisei Gakko grounds. This view was taken in winter after a slight fall of snow; but the snow melted so fast that I could not catch much of it with the camera. The small tower and building on the left belong to the Suruga Yashiki, or official headquarters of the province where I lived. In this yashiki, I was received by Katz and Okubo, and other officials of Suruga, when I first came to Japan.

Here a grand dinner was prepared for me in foreign style, and a reception given fit for a daimio. But, alas! I had dined heartily with my friend Dr.Veeder just before going to the Yashiki, not knowing of the culinary preparations made for me. Nevertheless, the banquet must be served, and my post of honor had to be at the head of the table. Etiquette made it essential that I should begin eating before any body else could commence. In vain, I excused myself in broken Japanese, saying that I had just risen from dinner. This was supposed to be polite affectation, showing that I had a delicate appetite. The more excuses I made the more I was pressed to eat. To decline was a lack of respect to my hosts, and a reflection upon the excellent cooking; besides, whenever I stopped every body else laid down their knives and forks, though I knew they had been waiting a long time and were very hungry. To go forward I could not, and to stop entirely I did not dare! Course after course came and went. The dinner was excellent, and served in splendid style, in dishes belonging to the Tycoon, which I afterwards used on similar occasions at Shidz-u-o-ka. Soup, fish, meats, and savory viands came in endless succession. I tasted each course and then stopped. Every body else did the same. I wished for an artificial stomach, such as Jack the Giant-Killer possessed when he ate more hasty pudding than the giant, and made the monster perform *hara-kiri*. Finally, the last dish disappeared from the table. My companions still felt hungry, and I felt like exploding!

Beautiful presents were then produced. The Tycoon sent me a superb gold lacquer lunchbox, with solid silver sake bottles. It was the most elegant box of the kind I ever saw, and was worth five or six hundred dollars. I presented a large picture of the Yosemite Valley to Katz, and a diagram of the new capitol at Albany to Okubo.

So ended the first banquet and reception at the Yashiki.

Chapter 9

A Peep into the Mikado's Palace

For long ages the Mikado of Japan has had religious reverence paid him by his subjects as the "Son of Heaven." He sat behind a screen at his ancient capital Kyoto, and no one might dare approach him except a few court nobles. His very existence was shrouded in sacred mystery, and neither his face nor his form could be seen, but only the voluminous folds of his imperial skirts. The military chieftain, the Tycoon, managed all the affairs of state during this time at Yedo. At last, after the revolution of 1868,[34]

---

[34] The Meiji Emperor ascended the throne — the "Meiji Restoration" that began the Meiji era (1868-1912).

the Mikado came forth from his seclusion and established his court at Yedo, which thereupon became Tokyo, or Eastern Capital. The Tycoon retired with his retainers to Shidz-u-o-ka.

Since my arrival at the capital I had been in- tensely curious to see the Mikado, of whom I had so long heard. I even planned to gain access to the emperor's palace, and see the whole of the imperial court and household, and in this, before many months, I succeeded. The lever that I used to pry open the doors of stiff etiquette and princely exclusion was the stereopticon!

I first gave some brilliant exhibitions of pictures at the Naval College for Mr. Katz, the Minister of the Navy; and afterwards at the Kaisei Gakko for Mr. Hatakéyama. These entertainments were attended by hundreds of officials and students, who of course were wonderfully pleased with the splendid stereopticon pictures of Europe and America.

Soon the fame of the stereopticon reached the palace, just as I intended it should! The empress and ladies of the imperial court were exceedingly desirous of seeing the beautiful pictures of western countries. But of course the ladies could not leave the palace; so I sent word politely to the lord chamberlain, through Hatakéyama, saying that I would come to the palace and give the empress an entertainment, and that the Mikado might come to the exhibition if he saw fit.

The offer was a novel one, as no foreigner had ever been admitted to the palace in such a way before; but my proposition was gladly accepted. My gallant offer to the empress and her ladies was amended, however, by the lord chamberlain, who said that the exhibition should be given for the Mikado, and that the empress and ladies might come in if they wished.

At an appointed day, I went to the palace with Hatakéyama, and selected the largest of the state apartments, as the most suitable in which to give the exhibition. I then asked the lord chamberlain to fix the most convenient date. He stepped out in the garden and consulted the Mikado, who was just about to take a walk. His majesty said that Tuesday of the next week would suit him; but if any important state duties interfered, he would let me know.

Accordingly, about eight o'clock on Tuesday evening I had my instruments set up in the palace, and the large curtain suspended from the top of the partition of the apartment. Two large screens were arranged around the instruments where the officers at first fixed them so as to shut off the seats intended for the emperor and his household from all the rest of us in the room. But as soon as they had retired to give notice that all was ready, I made a slight and quick change, and pulled the screens backward, so as to make the way clear for a larger picture on the curtain. I placed the Mikado's elegant chair in the little alcove, formed at the end of the zigzag screen, just to the left of my stereopticon, where he would have the finest possible view in the room. In front of his chair was a small table, covered with a rich gold-embroidered silk cloth; on his left was another table, and a seat for the empress; while in the rear were several lines of upholstered chairs, for the maids of honor and other members of the household.

A few days previous to the exhibition, I had requested Mr. Katz, of the Naval Department, to lend me one of the marine bands to give music for the occasion. On riding up to the gate of the palace that evening I met *two* bands instead of one marching up the hill; they formed in line in two companies, inside the gate, numbering sixty men in all, and began tuning their instruments for the exhibition.

After waiting some time for the foreign leader of the band (who was unfortunately detained by some misunderstanding respecting the passport of entrance to the imperial grounds), I placed the musicians in a side room near the large parlors, gave them directions to play the pieces appropriate to the foreign countries, the pictures of which would be shown in geographical order.

As soon as everything was ready for the exhibition, notice was sent to, the Mikado's apartments that all things were awaiting his majesty's pleasure. The emperor and empress were ushered into the room, followed by an impressive retinue, consisting chiefly of young ladies dressed in white, with their long, dark hair streaming behind, and broad red sashes encircling their waists; the effect was very pretty, and quite unique, as this charming procession of fair ones entered, and quietly seated themselves behind his majesty, while the band struck up the "Mikado's Hymn," and the word "Welcome," with the wreath of flowers, was thrown by the brilliant light upon the curtain.

The chief officers of the Kunaisho, or Household Department, sat on the opposite side of the room from his majesty. Tokudaigi, the lord chamberlain, and several other high officers were in attendance on his majesty; and every thing passed off in a very pleasant and social manner, there being nothing stiff or formal, though there was a subdued stillness in the room.

At the outset dissolving views were exhibited of Windsor Castle, Sandringham Hall, the Parliament Houses, and other English and Scottish places of interest, during which the band played "God Save the Queen." Then followed many American views of Niagara, the Yosemite, and the principal scenes in Washington, New York, and Boston. After this the magnesium stereopticon was started, and the magnificent views of Paris, Berlin, Switzerland, and Northern Italy were presented in brilliant succession.

Hatakéyama (who had accompanied the embassy in all their European experiences) sat near his majesty, and explained all the views as they were announced; designating, at the same time, the particular places visited by the embassy, and enlivening the occasion by little incidents of their experience.

The Mikado seemed exceedingly interested, and although every body else was quiet in his presence, he conversed freely and naturally, asking many questions upon places of particular importance.

After a hundred of the various well known scenes in Europe and America had been shown, interspersed with curious revolving chromatropes, and an ocean scene which was particularly impressive, a few comic figures were introduced, which created considerable merriment among the fair ones of the white-robed retinue sitting to the left, though they were very subdued and dignified in their expressions of delight and amusement.

The two bands of music played splendidly at first, but later in the evening, when the lights were down low, they lost their discipline a little, in the absence of the bandmaster. Some of them had seen the pictures previously shown at the Naval College, and told their companions how wonderful they were. The musicians were so curious to see the pictures that they could not stay in the room assigned them, but stole slyly behind the stereopticon to see the show. When I discovered them, they pretended they had merely come to ask what piece to play next! There were so many drums, trumpets, and fifes that half the band could make all the noise needed, while the other half came in to see the fun; and they performed very finely.

The exhibition lasted an hour and a half, yet the court wished it to continue longer. At the conclusion, I thought that my turn had come to secure the long-desired peep at the Mikado and the fair members of the imperial household. The room had hitherto been dark, so that I could not readily see the distinguished people about me. Only a broad cone of light fell upon the screen from the stereopticon. But when the signal was given for the Japanese servants to approach with their little paper lanterns, I knew the Tokudaigi had planned to remove the Mikado and his court from the room, without giving the foreigner time to have a satisfactory look at them.

Science came to my assistance, however. The punctilious lord chamberlain knew not the marvelous potency of the magnesium light. No sooner had the fair retinue risen from their seats than I raised the magic clock-lamp from one of the instruments, and shot a broad beam of white light, dazzling as the sun, down the long corridor through which the procession must pass. In an instant, the Japanese lanterns glimmered like fireflies, and the darkness of the corridor changed to daylight. The Mikado and empress passed out first, followed by the ladies of the court, who walked quietly, two by two, and hand in hand. Their dresses were similar to some of those I had seen in pictures of the ancient Kyoto court. The fair young faces turned one by one towards the brilliant light, which their curiosity led them to look at, and I noticed the little dots placed upon their foreheads, which designated the highest rank of nobility. Some of the ladies were very pretty; they wore their hair in thick tresses down the back, which style is only allowable for ladies of the court. Their eyes were slightly oblique.

The Mikado is a little taller than the average Japanese, with an open, fair countenance, having no decided expression except that of serenity. His profile is not very pleasing, but his forehead is high, and his eyes are manly and expressive. His dark hair curls a little at the temples. He steps with ease and carries his figure erect. On the whole, the Mikado is a sensible man and a good emperor, but as "a god" he is fast becoming a failure. His subjects cannot continue to worship one whom they see to be a man like unto themselves. In the picture (which does not do him justice) he is dressed in foreign costume, with gold-lace coat, broad epaulets, white pantaloons, military cap, and European sword. This dress designates him as commander-in-chief of the army, as well as emperor.

The Mikado issued an order that all the native officials and military men should henceforth present themselves at reviews and receptions uniformed in foreign style. Some of the Japanese ladies thought they would adopt European dresses also; but the emperor issued another order, saying that Japanese ladies looked well enough as they were, and did not need to change their native costume. Wherein the emperor was right. The ladies still wear the ancient style of dress, as seen in the picture of the empress. Elegant fans are carried on full-dress occasions by both sexes.

After the stereopticon entertainment the officers of the Kunaisho Department expressed much pleasure at the result, and said I must be fatigued and in need of refreshment. Accordingly I was led, with Hatakéyama and my two Japanese assistants, into the room where the Mikado's ministers are usually received. Here a table of refreshments awaited us. Cakes and confectionery, stamped with stars, leaves, flowers, and chrysanthemums, were piled upon the table, colored with all the tints of the rainbow. The confectionery was too artistic to eat, and I told the lord chamberlain that I would take it home to show my friends; he said certainly, that I might take it all, for this is the Japanese custom. I had frequently given dinners at which the invited guests carried away in their sleeves all the good things that were left! So there was no impropriety in my carrying away the sweetmeats from the Mikado's table.

The Tokudaigi said he had ordered one of the emperor's carriages to convey me back to the college, and that it would soon be in waiting. The carriage drove up to the gate of the palace in grand style, with two horses, two bettos well tattooed, and a coachman in full livery. It was evidently the barouche of the empress, and was luxurious within; my Japanese assistants enjoyed the ride exceedingly, for they had never seen such a carriage before.

We drove out of the Imperial Guard Gate, across a narrow causeway over a very deep moat, where Iwakura, the Mikado's minister, had been attacked by a dozen of the two-sworded Samurai, and nearly assassinated. He was badly cut, but saved himself by rolling down the steep embankment into the moat. The imperial guards were alarmed, and the would-be assassins were afterwards captured and beheaded. I subsequently dined at Iwakura's house, and found him able to walk with the aid of a crutch.

When our carriage arrived at the college compound it was nearly midnight, and the sleepy gatekeeper was inclined to grumble at being disturbed so late. But when his half-opened eyes caught sight of the Mikado's crest on the carriage, he fell on his face, and then flew to the bars and opened the gate quicker than he had ever done before!

The next morning all my instruments were sent to the college in the emperor's express wagon. A month after, a magnificent gold lacquer-box came to me with the compliments of the Mikado and the thanks of the ladies of the court. The latter said they felt as though the stereopticon had taken them on a journey through foreign countries, and that nothing in their seclusion at the palace had ever afforded them half so much pleasure. They would remember the occasion, they said, all their lives.

The, present sent from the Mikado was quite as elegant as the one formerly received from the ex-Tycoon, and was doubly valuable from its associations. The first gift - from the ex-Tycoon - represented the declining feudal power of the past; and the second - from the Mikado - represented a new era in the progress and enlightenment of Japan.

It is appropriate just here to say a few words respecting the various classes of society, which prevailed in Japan before the advent of foreigners, and of the distinctions, which are now slowly passing away.

In ancient times, society was divided into four classes. The first constituted the literary and military class, called the Samurai. The second, strange as it may seem, was the agricultural class, or common farmer. The third was the laboring class, or carpenter and artisan. The fourth was the trading or moneymaking class, the merchant. These were the chief classes that existed from 1604 until 1868.

The Samurai stood at the head of the social scale. He was the gentleman - the soldier in war and the scholar in peace. He could wield either the sword or the pen. Of the two, he rather preferred the sword. The sharp steel blades thrust in his belt were to him the symbol of rank and chivalry. He might walk the streets without a hat, but never without wearing his two swords.

In the picture representing the classes of society in Japan, the Samurai is seen standing on the left, with his long and short swords thrust in his belt. In the middle of the picture, sitting upon the ground, is the carpenter, who carries a square rule. The man with a book is a street storyteller and the girl on the right, with a sickle, is a farmer's daughter, who cuts grass, and carries it in the basket on her back.

The girl sitting on the left, with a musical instrument, is playing on the *Samisen,* or three-stringed banjo, which is more popular than any other kind of music. The strings are struck with a piece of ivory.

The man with a brick-shaped hat on the right of the group is a Ku-Ge, or court noble. Sanjo, the Prime Minister of Japan, wore such a hat when I first met him in Tokyo. The central and highest figure is dressed in the style, which once prevailed at the court of the Tycoon. But these ridiculous fashions are now nearly abolished.

The two ladies on either side of the highest figure are members of the Mikado's court; their hair is brushed back in the way I have already described in this chapter. Two dots upon their foreheads denote their high rank. All the other ladies have their hair dressed in the style of the middle classes of society.

The men have their heads shaved at the top, in the old-fashioned way. The Samurai have the family crests upon their clothing. Class distinctions are slowly breaking down in Japan with the incoming of western civilization. The Samurai no longer monopolizes the military power, for the government has called the common people to be soldiers, and the proud Samurai have been forced to labor honestly with their own hands.

It was my good fortune to witness a mock battle in the presence of the Mikado, showing the skill and discipline of the sturdy soldiers who now compose the new army. The battle took place in the suburbs of Tokyo, between fourteen thousand Japanese troops. It commemorated a peaceful victory in diplomacy, which Japan had recently gained over China, in the adjustment of the Formosa question, which had long threatened war.

On the day appointed for the battle the troops were drawn up in double columns at an early hour, and the two divisions were placed a mile or more apart. When the Mikado arrived upon the field, skirmishers were being thrown out by both parties; these gradually fell back as the two armies approached each other. The soldiers were all dressed in foreign uniforms, and armed with foreign Chassepot rifles.

The fighting soon became general. Double and triple lines of troops were ranged across the plain, and were completely enveloped in the clouds of smoke, which rose from their ranks. After two hours and a half of heavy firing and cannonading, the climax of the battle was reached by the troops of both sides becoming closely massed in face of each other, in front of a wooded hill-slope, beyond which the retreat could not be carried. Nothing could be more warlike than the scene now presented. For a distance of two miles the cultivated land was trodden down by thousands of feet, giving an appearance of sad desolation. Far away, a column of smoke was rising like a cloudy pillar, and the roar of cannon greeted the ear, like the sound of distant thunder. White wreaths of smoke overhung the woods, and the sharp rattle of musketry was deafening.

The last charge was like the grand tableau of a drama; and being in the midst of the smoke, and close upon the heels of the advancing line, I was favored with the beauty and excitement of a battle without the danger and sickening sights thereof.

Covered by the heavy fire of a friendly battery on a neighboring hill, regiment after regiment responded to the bugle-note, and lowered their weapons to the charge. On they went, sweeping across the plain, their long lines circling up from the right, and throwing volley after volley of bulletless smoke into the stubborn ranks of the enemy. 'The latter were massed at the foot of the hill, and unseen regiments were in the woods above; these opened fire by companies, and light lines of smoke drifted from the woods and scattered among the trees, like snow whiffs on a windy day. The wooded slope threw back ten thousand echoes, as the two combating forces closed upon each other. There was a rattle and roar loud and prolonged, and never did I imagine that mere rifles could produce such a continuous roll of sound. The shouts of the men and the blasts of the bugles mingled with the din and confusion, and clouds of smoke enveloped all parties. So thick was the smoke at times, that naught could be seen save the glitter of steel, and the bright intermittent flashes of the guns.

At last, the enemy succumbed. The clouds slowly lifted, and the cracking and roaring ceased. The line of battle on both sides broke up into various detachments, and wearily the troops trudged homeward.

Chapter 10

A Trip to Kyoto

Kyoto is the "sacred city" of Japan. Until a few years ago it was considered the spiritual capital, where his Mysteriousness the Mikado resided, whose august person was solemnly veiled from even the gaze of his own subjects. The idea of a foreigner from the outside world ever gaining admittance to the sacred city would have horrified the good Japanese of the olden time; nevertheless, wonderful things are happening in our day, and changes have come to pass which would have paralyzed the ancient court; so that I really went to Kyoto and sojourned among its most sacred temples as comfortably as though I were rusticating on the beautiful banks of the Hudson.

The Trip was a long one, requiring several weeks. I went to the port of Kobe by sea - a distance of 430 miles, and returned to Tokyo by the whole length of the Tokaido, on the overland route. The most interesting and historical portions of Japan were visited on the way, though I cannot do more than mention them here.

After some delay in receiving my passport from the Gaimusho, or Foreign Office, I left Yokohama on July 23rd, in company with an American friend and a young Japanese who had recently returned from the United States. We sailed in the Pacific Mail steamer Oregonian, which we nicknamed the "Roll-igonian" before we had been out many hours. The voyage only occupied a day and a half, but it was the roughest piece of sailing we ever wish to experience. The rolling and pitching qualities of the steamer were of the most unpleasant character, and as we were running through a very heavy sea, and there was no wind to steady the ship, our condition was really deplorable. I spent most of the time sprawling on the cabin floor; for no sooner would I crawl into my berth than I was unceremoniously pitched out of it again. My companions tried to sit on chairs; but in an instant, the chair-legs would go from under them, spilling them on deck and rolling them helplessly against the gunwale of the steamer.

The captain told me as we were coming into port that there must have been a typhoon to the southeast of us, which died away, leaving the sea in the dangerous condition in which we found it, with high waves and no wind.

The British steamer Bengal arrived at Kobé the day before us, and reported that she had never met such heavy seas, which were weathered with the greatest difficulty. A former Japanese friend named Nagai, who used to study at New Brunswick, and was now going to Osaka on business for the Treasury Department, told me that he had crossed the Atlantic seven times, but had never suffered from seasickness so much as on this short trip.

But even bad things have an end, and towards evening we came in sight of land, and steamed around a broad cape into the LV calm and shattered waters of Osaka Bay. All night we sailed quietly along the shore, watching the lights of the fishermen's boats glimmering across the bay. The sun was just rising as we rode at our iron buoy in front of Kobé, and fired the signal gun, which echoed and reechoed through the neighboring hills, telling the inhabitants that their mail had arrived.

We were anxious to reach the shore as speedily as possible after our misery on the "Roligonian;" *terra firma* never felt so good as when we placed our feet once more on land. It was early yet, and few people were stirring. So we started off and visited a renowned waterfall in a cleft of the hills behind the town. After a steep climb, we reached the fall, which tumbled from a height of sixty feet, making the rocky gorge reverberate with the noise and shock of its descent.

Kobé is very picturesquely situated between the mountains and the sea, and some of the foreign houses are very handsome. The town is merely the port and commercial outlet of Osaka, and is connected with the latter city by a new railroad.

We took the 11:30 train for Osaka, reaching the spacious depot on the suburbs of the city in just one hour. The cars are more elegant and comfortable than those on the Yokohama Railroad, and the locomotives are larger; both roads were built by English engineers, and the cars are small, in the English style. The Japanese conductors evince pardonable pride in the novel dignity placed upon them in collecting tickets and conveying passengers. They are very polite and competent however.

Osaka is the second city in size in the Japanese Empire. It contains a population of over 500,000, and is more compactly built than Tokyo. The streets are narrow and very crowded, but comparatively clean. So many large canals intersect the city that it might be called the Venice of Japan. Our hotel was conveniently located on one of these canals, and we made excursions from this point in every direction, exploring the sights of the great city. The shops were the finest I had seen, and were stocked with a great variety of goods; for Osaka is the commercial center of the country.

The three points of interest, which we first visited, were the imperial mint, the great castle, and the pagoda; from the latter a fine general view of the city may he obtained. The imperial mint was more extensive than the United States mint at Philadelphia, and quite as well conducted in every respect. We were politely shown throughout the whole establishment, and witnessed the moneymaking process on a scale we had never seen before. The mint is a granite building, and stands on the margin of the river; close beside it is a sulfuric acid manufactory, with a solitary brick chimney 150 feet in height.

We first passed through the rooms for melting gold and silver; here were small furnaces, containing red-hot crucibles. The melted metal is poured into molds, and cools in the form of long bars several inches thick. These bars are rolled in another room between heavy cylinders moved by machinery. It appeared strange to see the workmen forcing these bars between the rollers, as if they were only sticks of wood. They come out flat and bow-shaped, and are dark and discolored; the friction of the heavy rolling also makes them quite hot. Without thinking of this, and not noticing that the workmen had their hands protected by thick gloves, I attempted to pick up one of the bars from a freshly rolled cartful as we passed by. I dropped it quicker than I picked it up, somewhat to the amusement of those standing near, and concluded that money was sometimes a hot thing to handle!

The machines in the various rooms were very complicated and delicate: some were for punching the gold, silver, and copper coins, from the flat strips of these metals. Others were for rounding them off nicely, and turning up the edges; and finally the coins were placed in piles, and run through grooves to the stamping machines, which closed upon each one of them with a "bite," impressing the "dragon" and the value upon one side, and the "rising sun" and imperial crest upon the other.

We watched for some time the continuous streams of gold and silver pieces which rattled from the mouths of the various machines: at one point it would be a silver shower of dollars or fifty *sen* pieces: at another it would be a golden rain of five, ten, or twenty *yen* coins, bright and shining as the sun stamped upon them.

The new pennies, which had recently been put in circulation to replace the old *tempo* cash, were being produced at a rate that would have made the little boys' eyes dance; they flew out, of the hopper like chaff from a winnowing machine, and looked so bright that one would think them something more than copper.

The most beautiful instruments were those in the weighing-room, and the finest machine here was constructed by the Japanese. Each gold coin must bit weighed to see that it is of the exact weight required by the standard. In the weighing-room there are six tables of apparatus, brass levers, armatures, and scale-pans, all enclosed in glass cases, and all moved by delicate band adjustments, connecting them with the same power that moves the ponderous machines in the other rooms. The gold coins are pushed forward one by one, by feeders, to the delicate scale-pan, which acts automatically and almost with intelligence. If the coin is too heavy, it drops to one side; if it is a little too light, it turns off to another box; but if it is just right, it goes straight ahead to a kind of contribution box, which is usually better supplied than those for missionary purposes.

After visiting the mint, I was very much interested in inspecting the acid works. My companions could see nothing very poetical in leaden chambers and suffocating sulfur furnaces, even though they admired the big chimney, which is said to be the highest in Asia; and, in this chimney-less country, it is at least a consolation to know that the Japs have *one* chimney that even beats the average! I told them the consumption of sulfuric acid was the true standard of a nation's commercial prosperity, for it is used in all the processes of manufacture; and the acid works, with all their sulfurous fumes and furnaces, were a more reliable index of Japan's commercial condition than the glittering showers of gold through which we had just passed in the mint.

We did not forget to visit the great castle, which also stood near the river, and is remarkable for its high walls and deep moats, that once rendered it well nigh impregnable. But the towers and buildings were totally destroyed by fire during the fighting which took place here some years ago between the forces of the Mikado and the Tycoon. The walls and foundations are still standing, and here may be seen the largest blocks of stone ever quarried in Japan. They are quite as wonderful as those I afterwards saw at the Pyramids; but how the Japanese, with almost a total lack of mechanical appliances, could ever transported these blocks and placed them in their present position, I cannot tell.

While waiting at the guard gate for permission to enter, I measured one or two of the stones in the side of the wall. The first one contained over 500 cubic feet, and the others varied from twenty-five to thirty feet in length, with a breadth of fifteen or eighteen feet. There are no quarries near Osaka from which these massive blocks could have been taken, and it is supposed, they were floated up the inland sea, on great rafts from the province of Hizen. Near the top of the castle we found stone blocks still larger, a well 120 feet deep, from which we drew the purest and coolest water, with an interminably long rope. The view from this point is very fine; and near the castle was a cannon foundry, and government barracks, where 10,000 infantry and 3,000 artillery were quartered.

On our return to the hotel, we visited the new State House, built in foreign style, with Corinthian columns, spacious halls, and the whole surmounted with a dome! This imposing building was in strange contrast to the squalor and architectural poverty, which surrounded it. The interior is also a ludicrous mingling of the old and the new. In passing along the corridors I peeped into the compartments set aside for the various branches of government. Here were dozens of yaconims seated around tables, with piles of paper and bulky documents in front of them, while they smoked their tiny pipes and jabbered as lively as ever; they looked intensely Japanese, and yet all this was in a modern republican-looking Statehouse!

The last evening in Osaka, we took tea with Rev. Mr. Gulick and his family. Here we met Mr. Gulick's aged father, who had spent many years as a missionary in the Sandwich Islands, and had now come to spend his declining years with his devoted missionary son in Japan. The old gentleman welcomed me with special warmth, saying that he had read a great many of my letters from Shidz-u-o-ka, which were published in the New York *Evangelist.*

We attended the quiet Sabbath service which Mr. Gulick and one or two other missionaries held, in a private house, our last Sunday in Osaka, and were very much touched by the interest manifested by the few natives who came together to study Christian truth.

There is a river flowing from the vicinity of Kyoto and Lake Biwa, which empties into the bay at Osaka. It is customary to go up the river by night, rather than jolt all the way to Kyoto in a jinrikisha. The canals of the city connect with the river, and as our hotel was located near the main canal, we determined to take a moonlight trip to Kyoto.

Accordingly, we chartered a Japanese gondola, such as the natives used at Osaka, and transferred our baggage to it, adding a supply of provisions for the long journey, which we had in prospect after we should leave Kyoto. The sun had just set as our boat pushed off and quickly made its way up the canal; a soft haze slowly settled over the city, and as the full moon came out it gave almost an enchantment to the scene, and to the weird dwellings on the banks, which in sober daylight are none of the prettiest.

Continuing on a mile, we passed numerous bow-shaped bridges, the extravagantly high arches of which were more convenient for the mast of our boat than for the muscular ease of the jinrikisha coolies, who are obliged to draw their passengers over them. The bridges are quite a feature in this city of canals, and add not a little to the quaintness of the views.

The night had fairly set in as we reached the low but picturesque craft, which I have styled a gondola; it was waiting in the stream for us, and having transferred ourselves and baggage to the cabin-like place, which had been prepared for us, the boat moved up the river. There was plenty of space inside, though the cabin roof was scarcely four feet high; and stretching ourselves on the floor, to make up in length what we lacked in height, we looked out of the windows at the curious sights by the way. The evening was warm and pleasant, and thousands of people had gathered on the river in boats, to enjoy the cool breeze, in preference to promenading the narrow and sultry streets of the city. The surface of the water for a mile or more was covered with small crafts of every description. Some had old folks, smoking their pipes and taking their case; others had family groups sipping their tea together; others again had numbers of merry young people who were evidently out for a frolic, and enlivened the air with laughter, music, and talk. Each boat carried two or three lanterns, and some were decked with whole strings of light, with various colors. So numerous were the gay crafts that it looked like a moving constellation as they passed backwards and forwards. Now and then the small skiff of a fruit-seller would be seen darting in and out between the large boats, and the tempting array of melons and peaches, illuminated by a paper lantern, would be offered to the various occupants, who were already enjoying their tea and other refreshments. A few fireworks were let off on the river-bank by the juveniles, and the reflection of the hundreds of lights on the water gave a brilliant effect to the scene.

But the sight on our own craft was by no means the least interesting part of the entertainment, for scarcely were we comfortably settled, than the boat began moving up stream at a wonderfully rapid rate; and the mode of its propulsion was among the most novel and characteristic things we had seen in Japan. Eight men armed with stout poles, twelve or sixteen feet long, would start together at the bow of the boat, each with his pole braced against his shoulder; and then, with a yell, they would plunge their poles against the shallow riverbed, and rush together towards the stern, making the boat fairly jump on its course. On both sides of the boat, the raised gunwale of stout timber was cut with broad notches to fit the feet of the men, and, as they kept step with each other their nimble motions from one end of the boat to the other had all the effect of a machine. It was ludicrous to us who sat within to see this continuous procession of naked legs passing to and fro, for our windows being below, we could see the biped extremities of the human propellers with the least possible clothing.

However, they had a right to keep as cool as possible, for never did mortals work harder; and notwithstanding the difficulties of the current, and the shallowness of the stream, they tugged at their poles with a vigor and perseverance we have never seen equaled.

We continued up stream until nothing was in view but low meadows of long rank grass skirting the riverbank. Our men toiled on, pushing their poles with as much vigor as at the outset, until coming to a place where the bank was low and level they suddenly ran the boat close to the shore and jumped off; and while we were wondering what it meant to see all the nimble legs disappear at once, we felt ourselves impelled by a new form of motion.

We went on top of the little cabin to take a view of the situation, and found the men about forty yards ahead of us, tugging away at a long rope attached to a short mast near the center of the boat. This rope could be lengthened or shortened by a crank turned by the steersman, who with one hand guided the boat well out into the stream, and with the other accommodated the rope to the distance from the shore. It was a novel sight, from our perch on top of the cabin, to watch the men appear and disappear as they rushed along the path behind the tall grass and cane-brakes; sometimes we would sight another gondola, and then there would be a scramble and race to get ahead of it. There were some queer fouls in these races, but our boat always came out ahead. Boats from the opposite direction kept in the middle of the river, and were carried down by the current.

The night was still and clear, and the moon shone fall and bright; the cool of the evening was in pleasant contrast to the heat of the preceding day, and as we sailed quietly along, the scene was like a picturesque panorama. At midnight, we went below and crawled in the cabin window, where I stretched myself on the floor and was soon fast asleep.

I awoke at sun rising, and saw the poor donkey-men still shouting and tugging far ahead. The river was now quite shallow, and sandbars were on all sides. Though the boat was flat, it was difficult to make the few miles that remained. But the men worked well, either pushing at the poles, pulling at the ropes, scrambling through the grass and bushes, or jumping into the water, as emergency might require. I have never seen human beings labor more persistently than did these, eight men through this long night's toil, stopping neither to red nor to cat.

At last, we arrived at Fushimi, the suburb of Kyoto, where we disembarked, and took jinrikishas; it was still early as we rode within the limits of the Mikado's old and mysterious capital.

We spent a week in Kyoto, at a beautiful summer resort on the hillside overlooking the city; we visited all the points of interest, and enjoyed our stay exceedingly.

Kyoto, above all other places in Japan, is the city of temples, and to mention half of them would be out of the question. Most of them are large, and their grounds are laid out on a magnificent scale; many have noted historical associations.

The ancient palace of the Mikado, which has always given the chief sacredness to the city, is located within a large enclosure near the upper end of Kyoto; the grounds are in the form of a parallelogram, and contain a number of buildings with peculiarly shaped roofs. No other buildings in the empire are allowed to have this style of roof, except the shrines and temples of the Shinto sect. The Mikado was worshipped as the Tenno, or Son of Heaven; his head must therefore be protected by a Shinto roof, and his very residence became sacred. No paint was ever used about the royal dwellings, but the woodwork was of fine grain, and kept clean and polished. Sometimes the ends of the rafters were tipped with white, but this was the only color permitted, and gave a pretty checkered effect when used on the dark beams of the gateway and roofs.

Behind the palace proper is a large square garden or park also enclosed by walls, containing dwellings; here his Mysteriousness might retire if lie chose, and live a peaceful prisoner after giving up his duties of state to his successor.

All the interest connected with Kyoto, as being the royal residence of the Tenno, has of course departed since the removal of the Mikado's person and his capital to Tokyo.

Kyoto contains nearly 300,000 inhabitants; its streets are laid out at right angles, and are as regular as those of Philadelphia. Of the hundreds of temples visited, I will only mention that of "Kiyo-Midzu," or clear-water. This temple is splendidly situated; it was built about A.D. 798, and is considered among the most sacred spots in this neighborhood. It is approached by long slopes of stone steps. At the entrance of the temple is a pagoda, and along the edge of the buildings are high balconies or stages, which overtook the slope. The priests and people were at worship while we were there, and the beating of drums made a continuous din. The high stages are partially protected by projecting rails, as they overlook a depth varying from 100 to 200 feet.

Within recent times it was customary for eccentric individuals, who did not want to go to war, to come and throw themselves off this precipice, preferring to die before the temple of their deity, rather than be killed in battle.

Descending by a winding path from the stages, we came to the water-fall of the "Clear-water," which is divided into three streams by stone troughs projecting from the edge. Underneath is a small shrine in the rock, and hither pilgrims come to worship, and bathe in the sacred waters.

We took a bath there ourselves, but it was with difficulty that either of us could stand more than a few seconds under one of those solid streams of very cold water, which fell upon one like a liquid hammer. And yet, soon after coming out, we saw three men stand for eight or ten minutes, each with his head bowed forward towards the shrine, and the stream of water falling upon his neck and back, while he devoutly counted his beads, a string of which he held between his hands, and repeated prayers either for his own purification or for the healing of some sick friend. Sometimes persons will stand underneath this fall for a long time, as a kind of penance for sin; and even winter persons will kneel there, praying for sick relatives, till they are almost benumbed. The priests pretend that cures have been wrought, through the efficacy of these waters.

The largest bell we have ever seen in Japan was suspended near one of the temples adjoining our quiet hotel. The bell was made of fine bronze, and was more than ten feet high and nearly five feet in diameter; it was immovable, as all Japanese bells are, but was struck on the side by a suspended beam of wood, pulled back and forth by a dozen men. No sound can be more pleasant to the ear than the deep booming-ness of one of these bells; I do not wonder at the people love to listen to the solemn note, that may be heard on a still night for a circumference of many miles.

Our last evening in Kyoto was passed in watching the merry scenes along the shallow river-flats; here the people congregate in large numbers to mind the warm summer evenings. The riverbed is mostly a dry gravely waste, with streamlets flowing here and there through narrow channels. A fresh breeze may always be found here during the sultry evening, and numbers of small platforms or stout tables are placed in the shallow portions of the river, upon which the people sit and enjoy themselves. The tables are connected with innumerable restaurants, which line the riverbank, and busy waiters bring fish, soups, tea, and sake down the sloping walks to the guests.

The delicacy always in the greatest demand consists of fried eels, which are consumed by the dozen. I walked into some of the noisy kitchens where business appeared rather brisk; fires were blazing and kettles were steaming, while baskets of live eels were brought in and skinned, cooked, and served piping hot in an incredibly short time. The oily multitude appeared to enjoy their eel-feast exceedingly; and sake bottles were also emptied and replenished with marvelous rapidity, the boisterousness and merriment increasing in due proportion. It was the first noisy crowd I had yet come across in Japan.

But the scene was really brilliant, as we stood on the substantial brick-paved bridge which is the Nihon-Bashi of Kyoto, and which marks the beginning of the Tokaido. As far as the eye can reach, thousands of lights flicker and sparkle along the shallow river flats, and thousands of well-dressed people are trying to enjoy themselves. Each light or lantern is the center of a little group, and each group occupies its own little table, so that the great concourse is but a multiplication of social circles of every description.

Here sit half a dozen old men smoking their pipes around a brazier, and discussing the business items of the day. Here a cheerful farm group are seated, the father chatting with his neighbors of the nearest table, and the mother (busy as usual) mending some small fabric; the boys toss tempos, and the baby sprawls on the floor after an orange. Near at hand may be seen young fellows having a merry time with their "musumé" companions.

The fashionable young Japanese is quite a feature in his way. He sits with loose flowing dress, and sleeves tucked up at the shoulders, with a long-hilted sword in the background, gossiping merrily with the pretty lasses who look on him admiringly. The young "musumé" who gracefully on the table beside him is sweet pretty, but not loth to flirt a little by waving her long silken sleeve. She is one of the belles of Kyoto; is considered very handsome, and knows it. Her hands are quite small and white, and never did any thing more arduous than play the "kota" or "samisen." Her feet are clad in bewitching little socks cloven at the toe, and ready to slip into the bright lacquer shoes, which stand, on the stepping-stone. Her "obi," or sash, is of broad blue silk, fringed with golden lace and streaming down behind in true court style. Her little wallet is embroidered in rich fantastic figures, and her paper parasol is light and fragile as a reed. Her hair is done up in the most approved Kyoto fashion, which differs from that of the rest of Japan in being brushed up straight over the forehead, and after being held in place by sundry gold and tortoiseshell pins, projects several inches behind, over the freshly powdered neck. The face is fair and smooth, the lips brightly tinted, the eyes dark and slightly sad, and the teeth so beautifully white as to make the idea of blackening them seem horrible - as the married women often do.

Leaving this constellation of lights, which twinkle like myriads of stars all the way up the riverbed until far into the night, we wend our way homeward across the bridge, and through streets, which are decorated with flags and lanterns.

The neighborhood of our hotel abounded in teahouses, mineral baths, and places of amusement. Music and laughter could be heard on all sides, and as we retired to sleep, the merry prattle still went on about us. We were wafted off to dreamland, lulled by the plaintive melodies of old Japan.

We left Kyoto in the morning amid the bows and regrets of our kindly Japanese host and his family, and walked seven miles over the hills to the beautiful Lake Biwa.

I placed the young Japanese who was with me in a "*kango,*" as he was a little fellow, and might have been fatigued by the long walk. His name was Isami Kawamura, and he was but fourteen years of age; he had studied at Ann Arbor, and only returned from America two months before. He had evidently been a great pet with his schoolmates at Ann Arbor; and I do not wonder they fell in love with him, for he brightest and prettiest Japanese boy I ever met. He was full of fun, and it was quite an amusement to me and my American friend to get Sammy, as we called him, to entertain us in talking about the nice things he had left at Ann Arbor, for which he evidently felt homesick. He was full of the schoolboy spirit of frolic. He spoke English perfectly, and used so many droll expressions and American idioms, which I had not heard since leaving home, that his tongue kept us in continual good-humor.

As we journeyed over the hills he made us merry telling of his experiences with the boys and girls in America, and he said it was very hard for him to come back to Japanese customs, food, and mode of living after being used to such a comfortable American home as he had at Ann Arbor. The stout coolies who carried him in the kango listened to his lively conversation, and wondered what it all meant. He would joke them in Japanese occasionally, which only increased their curiosity.

On top of the kango in the picture is the flat straw hat sometimes worn by the coolies. These men are very muscular, and will carry the kango for hours without fatigue.

On arriving at the town of Otsu, at the southern extremity of Lake Biwa, we put up at a pleasant house overlooking the lake, and spent a quiet Sabbath here.

Monday morning we started up the lake in a tiny steamer built and managed by the Japanese; the boilers of these little boats sometimes explode, but fortunately did not do so on this occasion. Lake Biwa is nearly fifty miles in length, and is by far the largest lake in Japan. It is also the most beautiful. After sailing forty miles, we landed at Hikoni[35], a picturesque village at the upper end of the lake. Here we spent several days, making excursions around the lake and among the mountains; the view from the high castle of Hikoni is one of the finest in Japan.

The journey from Lake Biwa to the base of Fuji-Yama and the Hakoné mountain pass occupied one week, during which we traveled 350 miles in jinrikishas. It was a most interesting trip, but we encountered three days of severe rainstorms on the way, and crossed many small rivers. The longest journey was that which we attempted on the first day: we left Hikoni by moonlight, at two o'clock in the morning, and continued traveling until ten o'clock at night, arriving at the city of Nagoya, at the head of a large bay, which may be seen in the outline map. The distance traversed on this day was seventy-five miles; and that too on muddy roads, in jinrikishas pulled by men! Of course, we sometimes changed the men.

Nagoya is a flourishing city containing 120,000 inhabitants, and noted for its manufacture of chinaware, and elegant cloisonné enamelware, so much admired in America. Beautiful silk embroideries are also produced here and artistic fans. The Nagoya castle is very large. On two of the towers there used to be immense fishes made of copper, and covered with plates of gold. One stormy night a robber attempted in a gale of wind to mount into the air by means of an immense kite, and steal the gold scales

---

[35] Hikone and Hikone-jo (Hikone Castle)—probably the most beautiful castle in Japan—my favorite! DM

from one of the fishes! He was caught, condemned, and boiled to death in oil; the raising of large kites was afterwards prohibited. One of the fishes was subsequently taken down and sent to the Vienna Exhibition; the other I saw at the Japanese Exhibition in Tokyo. It was more than six feet high, with its golden tail upright.

Nagoya may be seen on the map, nearly ninety miles west of Shidz-u-o-ka, on the line marking 35 degrees of latitude. Kyoto and Lake Biwa may also be found near the same line some distance further west. (In reading and traveling, it is always well to consult the map of the country studied.)

We passed through Shidz-u-o-ka, wet and wearied, after four days of drenching rains and muddy roads; and a great many experiences I have not time to narrate. Beyond Shidz-u-o-ka, the rivers which I had crossed many times before were now swollen with the flood, and utterly impassable. So we chartered a Japanese junk and sailed across Suruga Bay. The junk had two masts and four sailors. A strong breeze was blowing, and we were soon scudding along at a rapid rate, under full sail. At first, it was glorious; but ere long the big waves came rolling in from beyond the stormy Cape Idzu, and we rocked helplessly in the bottom of the boat! Wind and tide had no respect for our feelings, and the farther we receded from land the more the breeze freshened.

We ploughed through the water, scattering the spray in all directions, while at regular intervals a huge wave larger than usual would strike us fairly on the beam, and for the moment, we thought we were going to the bottom. Jap boats are not very strong, and ours would shake and shiver as though ready to come to pieces; while ever and anon a shower of salt water would dash over the side to cool the situation.

More hideous than the noise of the waves were the shouts of the Jap sailors; the more the wind blew the louder they yelled, until they seemed like demons in the storm.

Finally, we came into smooth water, having made thirty miles in three hours. The scene was really romantic as our boat struck the beach on the upper end of the bay, and we jumped ashore. High and gloomy peaks surrounded us on three sides, and on the south was the sea, breaking along the rocky beach in low, dull swells. Dark and threatening clouds hung on the adjacent mountains, and night was slowly creeping on us; here and there, lights could be seen in the fishermen's huts.

An hour's climbing along the rocky cliffs, with the waves murmuring below us, and our narrow path lit by a single lantern, brought us to the open road leading to the city of Numadz. I was known and welcomed here; but it was eleven o'clock before we reached our hotel, and were fairly asleep. The next day we reached the familiar Hakoné mountain pass, where we found many friends from Yokohama.

Hakoné village had become quite a summer resort for the foreigners, and we remained here some time, enjoying the pleasant society and delightful excursions on the lake. When we entered the village after our long trip we were surprised to see American ladies coming up the shaded avenue of pines, dressed in summer costume and wearing bewitching sun-bonnets; they were the first foreign ladies we bad seen for some time, and we looked at them with delight.

The streets of the village were swarming with children as usual, and mothers carrying their babies on their backs stared at us with the vacant expression peculiar to the common people. Sometimes the babies had little red caps on their heads (as I have before mentioned), which I once mistook for "liberty caps," but which I found to mean smallpox!

Chapter 11

The Missionary Outlook

A few years ago, in journeying along the highways of Japan, the traveler would see at the entrance of every village and near the crossroads a wooden edict-board hanging where every passerby might read it, upon which was written in large characters, "The evil sect called Christian is strictly prohibited." This law No. 3 was suspended by the side of other laws against stealing, murder, and insurrection, and, like them, was formerly pu-nishable with imprisonment and even death. Why should the Japanese consider Christianity a criminal offence, worthy of punishment, when we believe it to be a blessing, and see in it the highest joy, love, and salvation? The answer is simply this:

In the sixteenth century, when Europeans first came to Japan, the Jesuit missionaries accompanied the traders, and succeeded in converting the southern provinces to the Roman Catholic faith. So successful were they, that a little later they entered into a conspiracy with some of the disaffected daimios, and attempted to overthrow the government of the Tycoon, and make Christianity the state religion. The conspiracy was discovered, and hundreds of Jesuits and Roman Catholic priests were banished from the country; a terrible persecution of the native converts also followed, in which tens of thousands perished by fire, sword, and crucifixion.

Christianity, so called, was swept from the land; its very name was written in blood, and children were taught to trample upon the cross. The edict-board, which I have mentioned, was written at that time, and placarded throughout the empire. Foreigners were expelled, and "the foreign religion" prohibited. The Japanese of later days looked back upon that bloody chapter in his country's history, and learned to associate the "Yesu followers" with ideas of intrigue, rebellion, and things worthy of contempt. He held Christianity accountable for the evil actions of the men who professed it; and he regarded the edict-board which daily met his eye as a righteous barrier against the dangerous sect.

Three centuries rolled away, when at last Commodore Perry's ships appeared and again opened Japan to foreign intercourse. As in former years, the missionary accompanied the merchant and trader; but this time the light of the pure Gospel of peace began to break upon the darkened pagan empire. American missionaries settled at Nagasaki, and afterwards at Yokohama and other ports; they did not bring the altars, candies, and crucifixes of the Jesuits, but proclaimed the simple story of the Scriptures.

Great prejudices had to be overcome, however, the name of Jesus had long been misunderstood, and the ominous edict-board still prohibited the "evil sect." Little progress was made at first, for the people were afraid, or openly opposed to the new doctrines. Even as late as the year 1872, Japanese who attended my Bible-class in Shidz-u- o-ka said they were astonished to find Christianity such a good thing, and so pure and exalted in its teachings, for they had been taught from childhood that it was evil and corrupt. They were so glad, they said, to learn that it was the true religion, of peace and charity, rather than evil.

Long and patient labor was required before this popular prejudice could be even partially removed. In the progress of events, however, the odious law against Christianity was taken down from the public highways, by order of the government, never again to be replaced. So great was the feeling of thankfulness and Christian exultation at this result, among foreign missionaries and others, that I obtained possession of the original edict-board which had so long hung up in my own Province of Suruga, and sent it home as a trophy and relic, to show friends in America the last vestige of religious persecution.

This weather-beaten board traveled eight thousand miles, by itself, and is perhaps the only one which ever left the country. After it had gone the local governor who had given it to me tried to get it back again; but I replied that Japan had no further use for the law, and that I had sent it to America for safe preservation!

The missionary work, which was slow and difficult at the outset, has received a new impulse within the past few years, and much good has been accomplished at the five open ports, and in some districts of the interior, which Christian men have been able to reach. As the provinces have not yet been freely opened to foreign intercourse, however, most of the missionary interests still center about Yokohama, and here many of the missionaries reside.

In March, 1872, Rev. Mr. Ballagh organized the first Protestant Christian church in Japan. The church edifice, now completed, stands in Yokohama, on a portion of the ground where Commodore Perry made his treaty in 1854; and the first thousand dollars given towards the erection of the church was sent by the Christian converts of the Sandwich Islands![36]

---

[36] Hawaii

The following year, in 1873, a Christian church was organized in Tokyo, on the same basis as the Yokohama church. Converts gathered by the missionaries of various denominations made up the membership of these "union" churches; and the Japanese wisely adopted their own method of church government, adapting their Christian polity to the necessities and circumstances of their own country. This independent course, which is the reasonable one, will be followed by other churches yet to be established.

Native pastors and evangelists are at present being trained in a Union Theological School just started in Tokyo. The only hope of completely evangelizing a country is by means of a native ministry who can preach the Word of God to their own people and in their native tongue. Foreign missionaries must lay the foundations, however, and may implant spiritual influences, which will widen and strengthen in coming years.

The most interesting and successful missionary work I found at Yokohama is that of the "American Mission Home," situated on "the bluff" overlooking the beautiful bay and harbor. The "Home" was established by three ladies sent out by the Woman's Union Missionary Society, and aims to educate and train Japanese girls in Christian truth, teaching them the religion of Jesus, which elevates woman to a position she has never been permitted to attain in the pagan countries of the East.

I often visited the Mission Home and enjoyed its kind hospitality; bright faces and a warm welcome were sure to greet the stranger at the door. It was a pleasure to see all the comforts and refinement of a truly Christian home placed on Japanese soil, and to meet groups of little Japanese girls, bright and happy, enjoying all the privileges and instruction, which love and Christian care could afford.

In the accompanying picture the grounds and main building of the Mission Home are given. The three ladies above mentioned are seen in the garden. Mrs. Pruyn, of Albany, is seated on the left of the grass plot; Miss. Crosby, from Poughkeepsie, is in the carriage; and Mrs. Pierson of Chicago, is seated at the side of the house.

Opposite this building is a new schoolhouse, not seen in the picture, in which the first Sunday school in Japan was established. The weekday school was also held here, which always opened in the morning with religious exercises. It was a very pretty sight to see the children gathering with their books and slates for school, and hear them sing the opening hymn in English, and then in Japanese. Mrs. Pierson accompanied them on the cabinet organ. The scholars were very smart at their studies, and compared favorably with Japanese youth of the sterner sex. Sometimes I brought down my chemical apparatus from Tokyo and showed them experiments, greatly to their delight. On questioning them afterwards, I found they always remembered the principles explained.

Adjoining the schoolhouse is another building of two stories, recently completed; here the smaller children and orphans are cared for by Miss Guthrie, formerly of the Calcutta Mission.

At the extreme left of the picture, Rev. Dr. Brown's house is seen, with a broad, sloping roof. Dr. Brown has been over eighteen years in Japan as a faithful missionary, and is at present associated with Dr. Hepburn and others in the translation of the Scriptures.

The noblest life work of Dr. Hepburn has been the preparation of the Japanese-English dictionary, which is an invaluable aid to students and missionaries in acquiring a knowledge of the two languages.

The missionary field in Japan is in many respects pleasanter that in other countries of the Far East, such as China and India. The Japanese are more sympathetic and cordial than the majority of Asiatic people, and the climate of the country is one of the finest in the world. The mission cause is in its infancy, however, and many laborers must yet be sent to sow the seed of future spiritual harvests. Noble men have labored here in the past, in the midst of danger and discouragement; and the record of modern missions in Japan, though brief, is filled with honest Christian endeavor and unselfish zeal.

A stranger might say, "What is the use of converting the Japanese people to Christianity?" It is often argued that they are well enough off in their present condition. As a people, they certainly excel us in politeness, gentleness, obedience to parents and superiors, and in social manners are our peers. They have also a culture and native refinement that surprises the foreigner; and their sense of honor is at least equal to that of the average American. Some of our customs, to them, are far from being desirable traits of civilization. The common people of Japan, with their simple wants and frugal ways of living, are at least as happy and contented as the corresponding class of society among us. Buddhism teaches them various virtues, restrains them from excesses, costs them little trouble or expense, and seems to meet their present religious necessities. Why, therefore, press Christianity upon their acceptance, causing them to relinquish all the sacred legends of the past?

Our reply is, that whatever culture may be possessed by the higher classes of the Japanese people, even their lives on earth would be better, their hopes brighter, and their passive existence elevated and quickened, by the incoming of Christianity. The religion we present to them is not a mere myth like Shinto, or a bewildering form of worship like Buddhism, nor yet a callous moral code like Confucianism. It is the very life of the soul; it breathes into men a new being, and warms the heart with a new glow of love to God the Father of all. In the face of Jesus Christ, it solves the baffling mystery of life, points to hope and happiness beyond the grave, comforts the sorrow-stricken and discouraged soul, and gives peace and even joy, in the midst of sufferings that all mankind are called upon to bear.

Above all, Christianity brings salvation. Leaving out of view the benefits and blessings derived from it in this world, it means deliverance from eternal death. This life is a very small thing, when compared with the life beyond; and the possibilities and privileges of that life for us, all center in the person and work of Christ. The Japanese belong to the same sinful, tempted, sorrowing race, as ourselves, and they stand in need of the same Redeemer. "And how shall they believe in him of whom they have not heard?" Or how shall they hear, unless the missionary be sent to proclaim the glad tidings? Christ's own command is, to carry the Gospel to every creature; and *he* well knew that every people on the earth had *need* of it.

We know not God's mysterious plan concerning the pagan millions who yearly pass into eternity, nor how far divine mercy and infinite compassion may be exercised in their behalf; but we *do* know that God's word commands us to carry the Gospel to every member of our guilty race, and that the divine presence is promised in so doing.

In glancing over a letter written when about commencing my bible-classes in Tokyo and when unusual difficulties appeared in the way, I find this statement concerning my students: "I confess that when the feeling floods upon me, that *these* are souls for whom Christ died, and *mine is* the privilege to make the fact known unto them, it breaks through all bounds of mere expediency, and forces me to speak the truth at all risks . . .. There is a solemnity beyond expression, in the attempt to bring before these young men the words of eternal life."

The very avidity with which the story of the cross was received by some, and the self-righteous air with which it was rejected by others, both served to show that at least grace and the Gospel *were needed.*

In Japan, as in every other country, some hear the word gladly, and believe; others listen with utter indifference, or openly refuse the way of salvation. At one moment the heart of the instructor would be gladdened by the words, "Sir, please teach us to pray by ourselves;" or, "Sir, these are golden truths, and we thank you for them." At the next moment, a curling lip, and a skeptical remark from another source, would show that seed was being sown on stony ground.

Light and shadow blend together in the missionary's experience, but still his duty is to "preach the word." I once saw this illustrated on a long trip with Rev. Mr. Ballagh, in our first attempt to ascend Fuji-Yama. We were passing through a village near Oyana Mountain, where a dread deity is said to reside. Here we encountered a procession of people dragging a huge cart with long ropes. Upon the cart was a pagoda-shaped tower, decorated with flags and streamers, in which were dancing men wearing hideous masks of foxes, demons, and ghosts. Drums were loudly beaten, and the people shouted to drive away the evil spirits.

As the people caught sight of the two foreigners the procession halted and the drums ceased, for we were great curiosities in this out of the way region, and even the dancing foxes looked slyly at us.

Mr. Ballagh was always ready to seize an opportunity for sounding the gospel trumpet; so, jumping upon a low balcony, he asked the people in a pleasant way what this all meant. They said it was the day set apart to propitiate the evil deity of the mountain, who sent all the woes and suffering upon the people, and little foxes to destroy their rice crops. This deity sometimes assumed the form of a great serpent, and naught could be expected from it but evil,

The missionary listened to their explanations, and then raising his voice said: "There is a serpent that brought evil into the world, and suffering upon the human race; but he does not live in yonder mountain, nor can his cruel power be broken by noisy processions or the beating of drums." Then with great skill Mr. Ballagh told the story of the serpent in the Garden of Eden, and the temptation and fall of man, closing with the solemn question, "Is there no deliverance or salvation from the power of this evil one?"

The people could not answer. Then he explained to them with great tenderness the wonderful plan of redemption; saying, that God had given a promise in Eden, which was fulfilled in Jesus Christ, and that now, all who believed on Him might be saved.

Immediately there was a division in the multitude; some were deeply moved, and wished to hear more, but the others beat their drums and called upon the people to take hold of their ropes and drag the cart and dancing foxes. The priests pulled the people away from the preacher, and the noisy but diminished procession went on its way, dragging with difficulty the heavy cart. A few remained and listened to the word with increasing interest, until I reminded Mr. Ballagh of the lateness of the hour, and we continued the journey.

A few days subsequent to this, I saw the same missionary go up to the open door of a temple, and by his winning eloquence, and fluency in Japanese, turn the assembly of Buddhist worshippers away from their idols. The next Sabbath the priests of this temple came to our hotel, and listened for two hours to an earnest presentation of Christian truth!

It would be a pleasure to give a lengthened sketch of missions in Japan, but I have not space to do so in this little work. I will, therefore, close this chapter with a few explanations of the accompanying plate, of the Lord's Prayer in Japanese.

It is a facsimile of Matt. vi : 9-13, in the gospel recently issued by the Translation Committee at Yokohama. The original of this plate was prepared in New York, by the American Bible Society ; and it is the fairest specimen of printing in Japanese that I have seen produced outside of Dai-Nippon.

In reading the prayer, a person should commence at the right-hand column and read downwards. Some of the characters are seen to be square and more compact than the rest. These are Chinese words, which are introduced into the writings of Japan in the same way that Latin terms are frequently used in English. In this case, each Chinese word is explained by a few simple Japanese characters, written in small type on the right margin. This is necessary to enable the common reader to properly understand the meaning.

The Chinese literature has been studied as a classic for many centuries in Japan; but only the Samurai, or two-sworded men, were permitted to become scholars, also the priests. The common people could only read the simpler forms of pure Japanese, which language remained quite undeveloped. In publishing the Scriptures, therefore, to the people, a difficulty arises from the lack of a suitable language, which may be equally well understood by all. If the missionaries translate the Bible with the frequent use of Chinese characters, it places it entirely beyond the use of the masses; though its literary merit is elevated in the eye of the Samurai, so that it claims scholarly respect. If it is translated in the purely Japanese dialect, it becomes simple and apparently childish, and has little merit with the higher class; in fact, it is impossible to properly express spiritual truth in a language so immature and so filled with crude mythological terms as the pure Japanese.

The translators are forced, therefore to strike a balance between the literary or classic language, and this simple but insufficient Japanese vernacular. This is accomplished by using as few Chinese terms as possible, and then explaining them in the margin so that common people may understand. Hence, the use of the small letters to which I have referred.

I wish this Lord's Prayer could be circulated in the country by thousands of copies, for it is a gospel in itself, and no tract more appropriate could be issued. Nothing appears less understood to a Japanese mind than the nature and meaning of prayer. This "talking to God" is a great mystery, and I was frequently called upon in my Bible-classes to explain, or attempt to explain, how we could reasonably and hopefully look to the Invisible One and say, "Our Father which art in heaven." Some of my students once asked me to please write a prayer for them; and what could better meet their wants in this respect, than that which came in response to the humble request of the early disciples, "Lord, teach us to pray."

Chapter 12

Farewell to Japan

Shortly after returning from the trip to Kyoto, I was called upon to bury my faithful servant Sam Patch. It was somewhat remarkable that he died exactly three years from the day I first engaged him, and that *my* contract with the Japanese Government expired about the same date. Though an associate of humble capacity, Sam was faithful in his own little sphere, and he was the only individual who remained uninterruptedly with me during my sojourn in the country. He had been unwell before I started on the Kyoto trip, and I sent him to the Tokyo hospital, where he had good care. But he was imprudent in leaving the hospital too soon, so as to have my house in good order on my return.

I sent him back to the hospital, and visited him one evening, and took to him the sad news that he must shortly die; for his disease - the "kaki," a kind of dropsy peculiar to the Japanese, was approaching his heart. The poor fellow was never very brave, and he cried a little; for he thought he was getting better. I tried to comfort him with his Christian hope, and then bade him good night. The next day he was dead, and when I came to the house where he had been removed, he was already placed in the Japanese coffin!

To give some idea of the Japanese mode of treating the dead, I will briefly state how Sam's remains were disposed of; but his case differs from others, in that I gave him a Christian form of burial, becoming his former Christian profession and the simple trust in Christ, which he seemed to have to the last.

Immediately after death, and before the body became rigid, he was placed in the ordinary square coffin with head bowed and knees doubled up and crossed in front, causing him to occupy a space so small as would appear incredible. When I first went into the room it was nearly midnight, and I had a flickering candle in my hand. Seeing a box scarcely three feet square in the corner of the room, I was told that it contained all that remained of poor Sam. Raising the lid, I glanced in and saw what appeared a shapeless bundle, with hand or foot projecting here and there; and this was the comfortless manner in which the Japanese usually bury their dead.

Sam's face, when raised, was calm and natural, and in his hand was a Testament which I had given him the year before, and which his wife had placed there to be buried with him, though whether at his request or not I do not know.

The little funeral occurred the following day, and I telegraphed Rev. Mr. Ballagh to attend; but as he was out of town, Rev. Mr. Thompson officiated, using the Japanese language. At the conclusion of the service, the hearse, which is a temple-shaped cart, five feet high, backed up to the door, and the sides and roof being taken off, the square box was pushed inside. The hearse was then put together again by piecemeal, and two old men drew it off, amid the sobs of some and the smiles of others.

Then came the queerest funeral procession in which I ever participated. Sam's wife and another woman were placed in a jinrikisha behind the bier; and then came my friends, Mr. and Mrs. Arthur, who had been very kind to Sam during his sickness, and finally Nakamura and myself brought up the rear in a third jinrikisha. Slowly this droll procession moved up the main street or Tori of Tokyo, attracting great attention, from the fact that no foreigners had ever been seen with such a curious structure as that on the cart, and the people were at a loss to know what such a funeral-train meant.

The place of burial was two miles and a half distant, and I tried to hurry the old men who drew the temple-cart. But they were either too lazy or too dignified to run, and the big cart was very heavy, owing to its large roof. At last, we moved on at a jolting rate that nearly shook the hearse and its contents to pieces. The road seemed interminably long, and it was dark when we reached the ground of the large temple in the suburbs of the city, where I had secured a plot, and caused a grave to be dug that morning.

I had intended burying Sam beside my interpreter Shimojo, who had died the year previous, and whose tomb was not far from this spot. But strict regulations had recently been issued respecting the burial of persons within the city limits. Therefore, I accepted Nakamura's offer to bury Sam beside the tomb of Nakamura's ancestors at the temple just mentioned, situated beyond *Kliristien zaka, or* "Christian slope."

Arriving at the temple, I stopped the hearse at the main gate, and hurried forward to see if the grave had been dug as I directed. Fumbling my way through the compact rows of ancient monuments and headstones, in the gathering darkness, I stumbled on the freshly turned earth, and found the deep square hole prepared as had been promised.

Coming back, I met Mr. Arthur who found that the graveyard was so cold and damp that it would be imprudent in his state of health to remain longer. So I thanked him and his good and amiable wife, and advised them to return, saying that it was too chilly for them, and I would bury poor Sam alone. (My good friend Mr. Arthur died of consumption only a year or two after this.)

Bidding them good night, I turned towards the temple, and was surprised to find it illuminated, and to hear a Buddhist service going on within. Stepping up to the porch and entering, I found a tastefully decorated apartment with mats and polished floors, and solemn-looking labyrinths beyond the dark line of pillars. Two finely robed priests sat upon a raised dais before the altar, intoning their prayers in a rapid and measured way, which struck me as being a funeral dirge; they took no notice of me as I stood in the shadow of the hall, looking on. The altar was a beautiful object, ablaze with tapers and shining with the gilt idols and golden leaves of the lotus lilies. Incense was burning before it in a bronze brazier, and the pleasant fragrance slowly filled the temple. But what attracted my attention was the white covered square box, placed directly in front of the altar, with a tall stick or tablet standing against it, having a name written upon it in Chinese, which I could not understand. Of course, I knew that this box contained a dead person, but *who* it was I did not at the moment imagine.

I was simply awaiting the removal of my own box from the hearse, and certainly intended no heathen rites to supplement the Christian service already held. But getting suspicious finally that "something was up," I stole by the priests and went silently up to the altar.

There, sure enough, was *my* box, with Sam's body in it, for it had the same bunch of flowers and bamboo reed upon it, which had been placed on the lid. My first impulse was to stop the service; for, without my knowing it, they had brought the body in, while I was in the graveyard, and had commenced their heathen rites as usual. As I afterwards learned, the *sinjo,* or present of money, which I had previously given the priests, made them polite and particularly anxious to do the thing up well.

As I looked at the priests, and then at Sam's wife and the other woman kneeling on the floor, who seemed to be taking great comfort in the ceremony, I thought I would let it continue, especially as we were the only persons in the temple. I sat upon a mat under the shadow of a pillar, and for once the Buddhist service seemed solemn to me. The priests intoned finely and earnestly, the little bells chimed in harmoniously, and now and then, a deep-toned drum broke the strain of the continual repetition of "Na-mi-ho Ho-ren-gi-ko."

I knew that Sam would not have highly indorsed this service himself, neither was it exactly compatible with the doctrines of the Testament within the coffin which stood before the heathen altar. Nevertheless, there was a novel interest in the scene, and as the service was soon completed, the chief priest bowed, and led the way to the cemetery, still repeating strange sounds, and wearing his silken robes. The bearers followed with the square box, which was safety lowered into the grave. The cemetery was lit up by the glare of the torches and lanterns; and as the priest retired I leaned upon a gravestone, and waited to see the grave properly filled.

A man was still in the hole, and I saw him striking the box with his shovel. On being asked what he was doing, he replied that it was sometimes the custom to break in the head of the coffin and fill it with earth! I told him he might dispense with that operation this time, and fill up the grave immediately, which he did.

Thus ended poor Sam's earthly career. His widow sent me a request for money to buy incense to burn before the tomb. Over Sam's remains, I caused a stone cross to be raised, upon which were inscribed the simple words, SAM PATCH.

My engagement with the Japanese Government was twice renewed at shorter intervals of several months, but as I did not feel that my life work was to be in Japan, I made preparations toward the spring of the year to start homeward.

I arranged to leave in March, as I supposed I could then accomplish my long-desired tour through India before the hot season fairly commenced in that country. In this latter respect, I was mistaken, however, for I fell into the very hottest season of the tropics.

On March 7th I met many of the students of the Kaisei Gakko, at a farewell gathering held in Dr. Veeder's house, as my own house was now in disorder with packing-boxes and trunks, and we all spent a pleasant evening together.

At the close I made the students a little speech, expressing my sorrow at parting, and giving them encouragement and hope for the future. I urged them to continue diligent both in their scientific and their religious studies, and to attend the Bible-class, which Dr. Veeder had now opened for them, and which would continue the work of Sabbath evening instruction.

They all seemed to feel deeply in reference to my departure, and also manifested no little awe at the formidable journey before me. One student, who was a most regular attendant upon my Bible-classes, but who formerly opposed Christianity, said to me, "Sir, we shall never meet again in this world, but I trust we shall meet in heaven." He then asked me to write my name and his own in a Bible and hymnbook which I bad given him. Another student said, "Sir, you have taught us great and beautiful things, both in science and in religion; and we are very thankful, and will never forget your kindness." Others said, " We wish you a happy time in your long voyage, and we know not where we may ever see you, but we hope *somewhere.*"

Such expressions as these were heart-warming, and showed that the Japanese students were still as kindly affectionate and grateful as I had ever found them during nearly four years' intercourse and instruction.

At the close of the evening, a short prayer was offered, and the students sung a hymn. The next day, my American friends General and Mrs. Williams gave me a farewell dinner, at their elegant residence near the Treasury Department. I then paid my parting respects at the American Legation, and started for the railroad station.

At the Tokyo depot, quite a little ovation was given to me, which was at once a surprise and a delight. Over one hundred students walked two miles to the station to bid me goodbye; they were accompanied by the second officer of the Kaisei Gakko, who made me a pleasant little speech. I told some of the students of the first scientific class that I should expect to meet a few of them in New York when I arrived there from Europe. The prophecy seemed like a dream to them, but it was fulfilled a year later, and they were really studying in the Columbia School of Mines when I arrived in New York.

It was a moment not to be forgotten when the space was cleared between myself and the cars, and I passed through the line of students and jumped upon the train. After bidding them a final "sayoonara," the whistle sounded, and half an hour later, I found myself in Yokohama.

The day following, Hatakéyama, the director of the college, came down from Tokyo, and gave me another farewell dinner at the Grand Hotel. He was very kind, and as affectionate as ever. I spent the last hour on shore in talking over "old times" with him, and in making plans for the future. He said that he would meet me the second time around the world at the Centennial Exhibition in Philadelphia, and that he would come *viâ* San Francisco.

He subsequently fulfilled his promise in coming to America, but I missed him by just one day in New York, and afterwards failed in seeing him at the Centennial. He was very sick at the time, of consumption, and started homeward shortly after-wards, viâ Panama. But he died on the Pacific, a few days before the steamer reached his native land; and though he was a member of the Christian church, he was buried in a Shinto cemetery in Tokyo, with the most imposing pagan honors!

Thus, one after another of my Japanese friends have been taken away by death.

The steamer Behar sailed from Yokohama at four o'clock. I was accompanied on my journey by Mr. and Mrs. Ballagh, and Mrs. Pruyn, of the Mission Home, who were going as far as Nagasaki to see me off. I also gave my chemistry assistant a trip to Kobé, and then sent him to Kyoto.

The voyage to Kobé was not so rough as the one previously described, and the sail through the inland sea of Japan was delightful. The passage of the inland sea occupied a little more than twenty-six hours, and was fully as varied and beautiful as we anticipated. It contained all the panoramic effect of river scenery with the vastness and solemnity of the sea. At one point it broadens into bays and gulfs, stretching away as far as the eye can reach; and at another it tapers down to such narrow limits that there scarcely seems room enough to pass. As one island after another was left behind it still revealed an open stretch of sea beyond, and each bay and inlet had so many branches, that it appeared an unlimited archipelago, combining the beauties of the country with the wildness and majesty of the ocean.

The provinces bordering the inland sea have always been populous, and in old feudal times, many strong castles towered in defiance along these shores. Some of their white walls and deserted parapets could still be seen, glistening through the dark-green foliage. Usually a large town or village would be seen nestled on the shore near the castle.

The eastern entrance of the inland sea is opposite the Osaka Bay, and is simply a narrow strait not a mile in width. The western or lower entrance is situated at the Straits of Shimonoseki, which may be seen on the outline map, opposite Korea. Our steamer stopped at the town of Shimonoseki some hours, and we all went ashore and rambled over the hills. But the place is of no particular importance, except that it was here that the old Japanese forts were located which fired upon certain foreign ships a few years ago, and thus gave rise to the "Japanese indemnity." No great harm was done, however, and our government had no right to force Japan to pay $700,000 into the U. S. Treasury.

In olden times, a very important naval battle was fought near this point by Japanese junks filled with armed men. South of Shimonoseki, the city of Saga will be seen on the map, where the insurrection quelled by Okubo occurred, and where he beheaded my young friend Katski. This minister Okubo has himself since been assassinated in Tokyo, and buried at the same Shinto cemetery as Hatakéyama.

At the southwestern extremity of Japan is the city of Nagasaki, which has been open to foreign intercourse longer than any other point. To reach this place from Shimonoseki we passed through the straits into the open sea, rounding a bleak and rocky coast, until we came in sight of the coal islands of Taka-Shima, which stand near the entrance of Nagasaki Harbor. On sailing up the narrow and cliff-girt harbor, we passed close beside the rocky islet of Papenburgh, from whose steep heights the persecuted Christians were once thrown into the sea. The harbor is a narrow arm of the sea, stretching eight miles inland and not more than a mile in breadth. It is completely enclosed by broken ranges of hills, diversified at the upper portion of the harbor by cultivated fields, shrubbery and trees, native houses and huts, foreign residences, myriads of junks, and all that characterizes a native and foreign settlement. Long lines of shipping usually lie at anchor here, including steamers and men-of-war. The city contains about 33,000 inhabitants.

I only had a few hours to spare at Nagasaki, for here I was to bid farewell to my companions. The afternoon was rainy, and I spent it in tramping around with my friend Rev. Mr. Stout, a missionary of the Reformed Church. We both wore rubber coats and boots, and with such an excellent guide, I soon visited the chief points of interest. We explored "Dezima," or made-land, a square enclosure of three acres at the water's edge, where the Dutch traders lived during the two hundred years in which they alone were allowed commercial intercourse with Japan. It was decidedly suggestive of the olden times to walk around these Dutch-looking buildings, and the stone warehouses which line the waterfront, and think of the sober, old-fashioned Hollanders who used to pace back and forth here at eventide, smoking their pipes, and watching for their ships from Holland.

In the suburbs of Nagasaki, we visited some very pretty gardens and summer residences, where I purchased a few pictures, while Mr. Stout talked pleasantly with the people. The grounds were laid out in the ordinary Japanese style, with goldfish ponds, footbridges, dwarfed trees, and airy pavilions, like that seen in the accompanying illustration.

Behind the native quarter of the city, there is a temple with groves and immense camphor trees. The trunk of one of these trees measured thirty-five feet in circumference. Here are buried five hundred and eighty soldiers, or nearly all of those who perished in the recent Formosa expedition. Most of them died in sickness, and only a few in battle. Their graves are ranged in rows of twenties and forties, and the regular lines of tombstones, divided off into sections or companies, present a sad and impressive appearance.

The last place visited was the Roman Catholic chapel, located halfway up the hill-slope, and facing the valley of Ura-Kami, where so many Christian converts were persecuted. The interior of the chapel is dim and solemn, and well calculated to impress the Japanese converts with awe. Near the altar were two colossal paintings, representing scenes of martyrdom at the time of the severe persecutions at Nagasaki. One of these pictures in vivid colors the crucifixion of some two hundred converts at once, upon the mountain of *Campeera,* "God of the sea," a bold bluff overlooking Nagasaki Harbor. Beyond this mountain there are boiling sulphur springs, called by the natives "Little Hell." Into a large open pool, boiling and steaming like a natural cauldron, it is said that Christians used to be cast who refused to give up their faith. With these horrible vats, and the rugged precipice of Papenburgh at command, the persecutors did not lack in natural facilities for torture.

But the hour for my departure drew near as evening came on. I took tea at Mr. Stout's, and spent the early part of the evening with my friends. Mr. Ballagh and other missionaries kindly gave me a "general epistle," commending me to the various missionary brethren I might meet on the long journey before me. Then I was committed to the watchful care of Providence, and amid mingled feelings of regret and hopeful anticipation I bade my friends farewell.

As I reached the steamer, all was quiet on board, and the raindrops were pattering on the slippery deck. The night was dark, and the wind whistled mournfully through the rigging as I went below. At early dawn, the steamer was sailing down the harbor, bound for Shanghai, China. The Japanese sun-flag floated at the stern, for the vessel belonged to the new Japanese line of the "Mitsubishi" Company.

I looked out of the cabin window at the murky waters of the Yellow Sea, and realized at last that I was face to face with all the dread uncertainties of a long and lonely journey around the world.

AFTERWORD

E. WARREN CLARK'S 1904 BOOK "KATZ AWA, THE BISMARCK OF JAPAN" AND HIS SUPPORT FOR JAPAN OVER RUSSIA IN THE RUSSO-JAPANESE WAR

Just as Clark's *Life and Adventure in Japan* reflects the feelings of many American writers during their first two phases of their modern relationship, his 1904 book on Katsu Kaishu [37], *Katz Awa, "The Bismarck of Japan"* vividly portrays the intensely pro-Japanese feelings shared by many leading Americans during the Russo-Japanese war. Clark embraces Katsu, his former patron and mentor, as a metaphor for the new Japan.

We know very little about Clark's activities between 1875 and 1895 except that he married, had numerous children, and devoted himself to his career as an Episcopal priest in upstate New York. He visited Japan on holiday in 1895 and 1904. Clark's letters to Griffis in 1895 indicate a much more positive and less critical attitude toward Japan than he had in the 1870s. He noted, for example, that "Japan is a good place to live in and a respectable place to die in, and almost wish that I was back here for good."[38]

---

[37] Katsu Awa (Kaishu; Rintaro; 1823-99) studied science under the Dutch at Nagasaki and was the Tokugawa Shogunate's leading naval expert in the 1860s. He was an advocate of the concept of *fukoku kyohei* (enrich the country; strengthen the army) in the early Meiji period. He had strong links with the Tokugawa shogunate and negotiated the surrender of Edo (Tokyo) in 1868. He was appointed to naval and other posts in the Meiji government, eventually attaining cabinet rank.

[38] Clark letter to Griffis, 17 November 1895.

During the Russo-Japanese War Clark helped to establish the War Orphan's Fund in the United States for American Sunday School children in order to help Japanese children whose fathers perished in the war. He wrote the short biography, *Katz Awa, "The Bismarck of Japan"* to enhance American awareness of the Russo-Japanese War, but the book is in reality an idealized portrait of Japan as a nation. His hoped to use all profits from the book as a means of raising money for this fund.

Although the thrust of the book is unmitigated praise for the deceased Katsu Kaishu, Clark states that he wrote the book in response to speeches and letters by his friend, noted Japanese statesman Viscount Kaneko Kentaro. Clark devotes considerable space to coverage of Kaneko Kentaro's wartime propaganda trip to the United States. Kaneko, an 1878 graduate of the Harvard Law School and later Professor of Law at Tokyo University, headed a propaganda mission to the United States to drum up support for Japan. He gave speeches at Harvard, Yale and other institutions. Clark quotes Baron Kaneko's 1904 speech at the Japan Club at Harvard University [39] where he

---

[39] The *Yale Daily News of* March 8, 1905 advertised Kaneko's speech to the campus that night:

WAR LECTURE TONIGHT
By Baron Kentaro Kaneko——The Situation in the Far East
Baron Kentaro Kaneko of Tokio, Japan, will deliver an lecture in the University Course tonight at 8:00 in Lampton Lyceum. His subject will be "The Situation in the Far East."

There are few men more capable of dealing with the issues of the present Russo-Japanese war than Baron Kaneko. He is a distinguished Japanese statesman, and a member of the "war" party in his country's politics. He was educated in this country, graduating from the Harvard Law School in 1878, and later became Professor of Law in the Imperial University of Tokio. The opinions of a man so closely connected with the present Eastern crisis cannot fail to arouse interest. He will give special prominence to an analysis of the causes of the war.

Yale Daily News, March 9, 1905
Baron Kaneko's Lecture
Baron Kaneko of Tokio, Japan, delivered a most interesting lecture in Lampton Lyceum last evening, taking for a subject, *The Situation in the Far East.* In spite of the inclement weather, a large audience was in attendance.

The speaker was introduced by President Hadley and he opened his address by taking the opportunity to express, in behalf of his country, the gratitude they feels toward Yale for the excellent statesmen and leaders educated in New Haven. He then took up a short history of Manchuria during the last fifteen years. At the end of war between China and Japan, in 1895, Japan was in possession of Manchuria, but Russia claimed that Japan's possession of this territory would be a menace to the East. This theory was also advanced by German and France, with the result that Japan was forced to abandon Manchuria in favor of Russia. A new menace thus arose.

In 1893 Russia made a secret agreement with China and obtained Port Arthur as a naval base. In the same year she was granted another concession, which enabled the extension of the Siberian railroad to Port Arthur. Attempts were also made to establish a naval base in Corea [Korea], as well as the ones at Port Arthur and Vladivostok. It was at this point that Japan began to see through Russia's maneuvers. However, her every advance was blocked by Russia, and after many attempts for peace, Japan declared war on February 4, 1904. From the beginning of the war Japan has **strictly respected international law**, and in order to carry this out, **two lawyers have been detailed to every regiment and warship** to decide any questions which might arise. Thus far Japan has upheld the international rules of war, while Russia has been guilty to a large degree. As a contrast between *Russia's "Christianity" and Japan's "barbarism,"* he cited the case of the ship Ruric which, while cruising last Summer, met a Japanese transport with 700 souls abroad. The Ruric fired on the ship and, as it sank, instead of offering aid to the drowning, fired on them in the water. Three months later the Ruric was met and sunk by the Japanese squadron under Kamimura, but instead of paying them back for their cruelty, the Japanese carried all as prisoners of war to Japan.

In closing, he described the daily routine of the Japanese soldiers and sailors, paying special attention to the way in which patriotism and courage is developed. Finally, Russia, France and Germany form a combination favorable to the pleaded for American help, both moral and financial, by portraying Japan as the progressive force for Anglo-Saxon civilization in East Asia:

> The very school children hoarding up their money and the pittance with which to purchase books, have carried these as offerings to the [Japanese] treasury department. The war will be long and terrible, and we realize it. This is shown by the fact that when a soldier or sailor is sent to the front, his family is taken care of by his neighbors or by the village community. Landlords make it a rule to collect no rent from his family, and doctors treat the sick family free of charge.

> In anticipation, also of many thousands of widows and orphans who must be left behind, a relief fund association has been established among the people themselves, who out of their poverty have contributed 1,300,000 yen. This war is neither racial nor religious in character. It is a battle for Japan's national existence; a struggle for the advancement of Anglo-American civilization in the East, and undertaken to insure the peace of Asia. To call Russia "Christian" and Japan "pagan" in this crisis is reversing the story of the Good Samaritan.[40]

Kaneko continued to press his point that Japan's behavior in the war is far more Christian-like than that of the regressive and ill-mannered Russian army:

> [Remember] the story of a certain man who went down, to Jericho, and fell among thieves, who left him wounded, stripped,

---

division of China, while England, the United States and Japan form a combination which upholds the "open door " policy, so that the war becomes not one between nations, but one between the liberal policy and militarism.

[40] Quoted in Clark, *Katz,* pp. 70-73.

and bleeding. The professional priest and Levite [Russian-like in their treatment of their wounded foes] "passed by on the other side." Whereupon the despised Samaritan, in the person of the "pagan" Japanese, comes along dismounts, and binds up the wounds of even his enemy. And the narrator says, in perfect truth, that the performer of the Christian-like deed, and he who is obedient to the Christ command, "Go thou and do likewise," is the one who loves his neighbor, and comes nearest to the standard set by Christ himself.[41]

Clark responds to Baron Kaneko's plea:

Japan has passed the darkest days of her religious history, and the brightest beams of spiritual light are yet to emanate from the land of the sun rising. The latent qualities for the intensive Christian life are there. Were I to seek conditions where the Holy Spirit delights to dwell, and where Pentecostal surprises, "as of the sound of the mighty rushing wind" are to be expected, I would seek it in Japan. I discovered more of the Spirit's presence and power in teaching His own WORD on the matted floor of that old Buddhist temple, where Katz placed me, than I ever found in Christian pulpit or cushioned pew. My necessity was God's opportunity, and when He brings us to "the end of the rope," in difficulties of language, discipline, and danger, or, later on perchance, into the deeper shades of our own Gethsemane, we learn adoringly who He is and whom we serve.

Not only in Dai Nippon, but in America I have used Japanese evangelists with marked success, for their sincerity of belief, earnestness of utterance and evident companionship with God gave them

---

[41] Ibid.

results in winning those whom some of us ministers had failed to reach. Japan is the freshest field of the Spirit's power today, and God will show what wonders He can do among the children.[42]

Clark wrote the biography of Kaishu to enhance American awareness of the Russio-Japanese War, but the book is in reality an idealized portrait of Japan as a nation. For Clark, Katsu stood as a model of what Japan is and potentially could be. Japan, like Katsu, was latently Christian. The qualities of a good Christian were already there deep inside the Japanese personality and it was only a matter of time before Japan became openly and truly Christian. Just as Japan was so busy emulating the West in terms of building modern railroads, a very modern educational system, and battle ships to destroy the fleet of "Mother Russia," Japan would eventually take up the Christian cause. Thus, it was the duty of Clark and other Christian Americans to continue to support and cherish Japan until it could save itself.

Clark was convinced that Katsu had become a covert Christian before his death —how else could one explain his very "Christian-like" behavior. Clark quotes a letter he received from Clara Whitney Kaji, a prominent American in Japan, just before his friend's death:

> A week or two before Count Katz Awa's death, my brother heard from his lips a clear confession of personal belief in Christ. It gladdened our hearts..... Some time previous...he would refer to Christianity pleasantly, adding in his characteristically humorous way, that he hardly dared to make a public confession of his faith, for fear the missionaries would make him "preach all the time." He was no Buddhist in these last days, even though he was buried with the impressive Buddhist ritual. His was a state funeral, and the family had nothing to say about it.[43]

---

[42] Ibid., pp. 77-78.
[43] Ibid., p. 88.

Clark implies that just as Katsu Kaishu had become a Christian upon his death, Japan too would eventually become Christian. As evidence that Japan was a nation that could change rapidly for the good and would rid itself of its pagan backwardness in a hurry, Clark cited the tremendous scientific, industrial, and technological modernization that Japan had experienced since the 1860s. Clark quotes an article by George Kennan, an American journalist in the American journal *Outlook* about Japan's surprising success in the early stages of the Russo-Japanese War:

> Imagine my surprise. Here I saw a people who, fifty or sixty years ago were using medieval weapons and sailing the seas in junks. They could paint enamel, make porcelain, cast small bronzes, etc., but no one could have credited them with doing things in a big way. Then, therefore, I find them creating great steel plants and gun foundries, making 13 inch rifled cannon, building war ships, constructing huge dry docks, employing 15,000 skilled workmen in a single establishment, and managing, without foreign assistance, the most complicated and ponderous machinery, my feeling is naturally of surprise."[44]

Clark agreed with Kennan and added:

> But it was the same physically fragile Katz Awa, who in those old "junk" days, was building the precursors of these things and prearranging the advent of bigger ones at Kobe and old Yedo. He it was in 1896 gave me the permit admitting me to that revelation of naval strength, "Yokosuka," on the bay south of Yokohama, where buildings like those of the Brooklyn Navy Yard astonished me, where a

---

[44] Ibid., p. 42.

white squadron (now gray) lay at anchor equal to our own, and where I went aboard the captured Chinese warship "Chin Yen," which was being repaired in the largest stone drydock I had ever visited. To see these pigmy Japanese lifting a massive steel turret from the deck of the battleship as a cheesebox on the shore made me think of "Gulliver's Travels." But who was the Gulliver, I didn't know.[45]

It is sad that Clark died in 1907 just as the first signs of friction between Japan and the United States were becoming evident. His beloved friend Griffis continued his active scholarship almost until his death in 1928.

---

[45] Ibid/, pp. 42-43.

About the Author

Daniel A. Metraux is Professor of Asian Studies at Mary Baldwin College in Staunton, Virginia. He has studied at Waseda University and Tokyo University in Japan and has a PhD from the Dept. of East Asian Languages and Cultures, Columbia University (1978). He has also taught at Doshisha Women's College in Kyoto, Japan and at Bentley College in Boston. He has written many books including *Taiwan's Political and Economic Growth in the Late Twentieth Century* (1991), *The Soka Gakkai Revolution* (1994), *Aum Shinrikyo and Japanese Youth* (1999) and *The International Expansion of a Modern Buddhist Movement: The Soka Gakkai in Southeast Asia and Australia* (2001). He has contributed numerous articles to such journals as *Asian Survey* and *The Japanese Journal of Religious Studies* and chapters to a number of books including Bryan Wilson, *Global Citizens: The Soka Gakkai Buddhist Movement in the World* (Oxford; 2001).

Jessica D. Puglisi is an honors student at Mary Baldwin College majoring in Asian Studies and International Buddhism. She is an expert in debate.

Bibliography

Burns, Thom. "America's 'Japan': 1853-1952 in *Kyoto Journal* (40) 1999, pp. 26-39.

Gulick, Sydney. *The White Peril in the Far East* . New York, 1905.

Henning, Joseph M. *Outposts of Civilization: Race, Religion and the Formative Years of Japanese-American Relations.* New York: New York University Press, 2000.

Iida Hiroshi. *E. W. Kurakucho 'Nihon ni okeru Seikatsu to Kiken* (E.W. Clark's Life and Adventure in Japan. Shizuoka: Shizuoka-ken Eigakushi Shiryo, 1955.

Ion, A. Hamish. "Edward Warren Clarkl and Early Major Japan: Case Study of Cultural Contact" in *Modern Asian Studies* II.14 (116), 1975, p. 178.

Perry, John C. et al., *Sentimental Imperialists: The American Experience in East Asia.* New York: Harper and Row, 1981.

Varley, H. Paul. *Japanese Culture*: (New York: Columbia Univ. Press, 1977.

Watanabe Masao, "E. W. Kuraku: Beikokujin Kagaku Kyoshi" (E. W. Clark:American Science Teacher in Japan) in *Kagaku Kenkyu* II.14 (116), 1975, pp. 174-84.

0-595-21587-4